The Book of
TOLE & DECORATIVE
PAINTING

Priscilla Hauser

PRENTICE HALL PRESS • NEW YORK

ACKNOWLEDGMENTS

I would like to express my gratitude to the following: Sheila Ross of Shiva, Incorporated; Bob Simmons of Robert Simmons, Incorporated; Jim Harkness of Color Photography, Incorporated; Juanita Scott, my Project Coordinator; Marynell Snow, Editor of Priscilla Hauser Publications.

I shall be forever grateful to my family, friends, students, and business associates for the encouragement, cooperation, and assistance that they have given me in all my ventures. Their love is the most precious part of my life.

First Prentice Hall Press Edition, 1986
Published by Simon & Schuster, Inc.
Gulf + Western Building
One Gulf + Western Plaza
New York, NY 10023

Originally published by Van Nostrand Reinhold Company

PRENTICE HALL PRESS is a trademark of Simon & Schuster, Inc.

Library of Congress Cataloging-in-Publication Data

Hauser, Priscilla.
   The Priscilla Hauser book of tole and decorative painting.

   Includes index.
   1. Tole painting.   2. Painting.   3. Design, Decorative—Plant forms.   I. Title.
TT385.H38   745.7'2   77-4767
ISBN 0-671-60907-6
       0-671-60908-4 (pbk.)

Manufactured in the United States of America

10 9 8 7 6 5 4 3 2 1

Other books by Priscilla Hauser
Dimensional Glass, Book I, 1971
Dimensional Glass, Book II, 1971
Rub Out Painting, 1972
For Whom the Brush Toles, Volume I, 1973
For Whom the Brush Toles, Volume II, 1974
For Whom the Brush Toles, Volume III, 1976
Make Mine Country Style, 1975
Priscilla Hauser's Workbook (published four times a year), 1973, 1974, 1975, 1976, 1977
Priscilla Hauser's Idea Book, 1977
The Collection Series, Volume I, *Daisies*, 1977
The Collection Series, Volume II, *Strawberries*, 1977

Contents

1-1.

Priscilla Hauser

I can teach you to paint! Now wait a minute—I know what you are thinking: "That gal is nuts. I can't paint. That takes talent." If you are one of the poor misled people who believe this, please believe me when I say you are wrong. All you need to say to me is, "I wish I could." Painting is like anything else: it can be learned, and, furthermore, it is not hard. Painting is no different from cooking, sewing, or playing a musical instrument. There is a sad misconception of art in our society today, because people think that it is necessary to have talent to paint. That's nonsense!

Stop and think. If a paintbrush had been placed in your hand instead of a pencil when you were a child, you'd use that paintbrush beautifully today. Remember that a paintbrush is just another tool of communication and is not difficult to use.

As an example, my husband Jerry and I have four children. They all paint; they are not afraid of a paintbrush because they have been brought up in a home where their mother paints. We always have paints and brushes out on a table, and to our children painting is just a part of life that is fun. I must admit that none of our children can cook; I don't cook either—just paint!

How I wish I could put into words what painting can mean to you. It is a joy, it is time filled with happiness that will last your life through.

There is another mistaken idea about art: that one must study it from childhood in order to be able to paint. That is absolutely false! No matter how old you are, I *can* teach you to paint. I didn't study art in college: I studied dental hygiene, because my father felt that I should have what he called an insurance policy—a way to support a family if necessary.

It is true that painting has interested me since I was a child. When I was in the seventh grade, a dear friend of mine received a gorgeous set of bedroom furniture from her parents. It was French in design. The twin beds, dresser, and little camelback trunk were white, trimmed in gold, and roses were painted on everything. I asked my mother and father

for furniture just like it, but they felt that it was too expensive for a young girl's room.

The following Christmas my parents gave me a beautiful camelback trunk, but it was unpainted. I went to the artist who had painted my friend's furniture and asked if she would teach me to paint. Her answer was "no," but in that conversation she referred to that type of decoration as tole painting. At age 12 tole painting became a part of my vocabulary. I asked everyone I knew where I could take lessons in tole painting, but no one knew. A few decorators in town sold tole lamps and trays, but, alas, there was no one to study with.

Years later, after Jerry and I were married, I longed to paint that little trunk for our home. We moved from Dallas to Kansas City, and, to my amazement, I found classes in tole and decorative painting at the YMCA and other recreation centers. I studied there for a few short months, learning all I could about tole and decorative painting, before we moved from Kansas City to Tulsa. We bought our first home, and I began to paint the wonderful collection of junk that we'd been accumulating for years: milk cans, coffee pots, waste-paper baskets, and, yes, my little trunk, which I painted with pears and grapes and gave to my mother the following Christmas.

My painting continued. Neighbors saw what I was doing and asked me to teach them to paint. This sounded like a good way to make a little extra money. I felt that, if people paid me, I must have something to offer them, so I began trying to figure out the best ways to teach them to paint. If I have any God-given talent, it is the ability to teach. Perhaps this talent developed because I have a beautiful sister who is without sight. All of us at home communicated things to her, since she was unable to see them.

As I painted, I made notes on everything I did and began developing methods, or recipes, for painting, just as for cooking. My first class had 6 students and was held in the garage of our home. Before I realized it, my classes had grown: I had about 35 students.

One day, to my dismay, I received a telephone call from the

zoning board, telling me that I was running a business in a neighborhood that was not zoned for business, that I would have to give up my classes or find a business location. Dismayed but not defeated, I went to a local paint store. The manager was delighted to stock the artist's supplies and materials I needed and made a small studio space available to me in the back of the store. Classes continued to grow, but then the manager of the store was transferred.

This was my opportunity to make a break and open my own business without stepping on any toes. Jerry thought I had lost my mind. "What do you want to go into business for?" he asked. "You are 22 years old and don't know a thing about business. You have a young family to raise. A business is a nightmare; you'll be working day and night." That did it. When anyone tells me that I can't do something, I'll break my neck to see that it is done and done well.

I borrowed some money from my mother, who had always felt that I could succeed. Jerry found a little old house that had been an antique shop. We rented it for $50 a month, and the Little Red Tole House was born. All my students worked to establish the Little Red Tole House, but the efforts of one person in particular stand out in my mind. My long-time student and friend, Lucille DeWitt, brought her husband Don to the Tole House who, along with other students, worked day and night knocking out walls, painting, and laying floors. It was July, the temperature was 105°, and we didn't have air conditioning. I'll always be grateful to those friends. That is another wonderful thing about this world of painting. It opens the door to so many new friends, people who share a common interest.

Classes continued to grow at the Little Red Tole House, and Noreen Banes—who to this day is my right hand—joined my staff as a teacher. Money received from classes was reinvested in inventory. I had 275 students a week and was teaching three classes a day. My business demanded so much of me that I was exhausted, but I loved it. By this time my husband started to take a different view of things. In the beginning he had said that I'd never make a go of it, and I must admit that my operation was not very businesslike at times.

I'll never forget the afternoon that two men from the tax department called on me. I was teaching a class at the Tole House when they asked to speak to me in private. Frightened to death, with no idea what they wanted, I told them that I had no office but that we could go to the bathroom. They

1-2.

6

looked amazed, and I explained that the tub was covered with wood and served as a table where salesmen showed me their wares. They did not wish to go to the bathroom with me and said so. They decided to return at three when class was dismissed.

Three o'clock found a surprise birthday party for one of the students in full swing, complete with a blazing birthday cake. The tax men returned to find wall-to-wall females, with the crowd getting larger and louder by the minute. In desperation they agreed to meet me in the bathroom. One of them sat on the board covering the tub, and I tried to hide my terror by graciously lowering the lid to the toilet and offering the other man a seat. He accepted with obvious reluctance: I can't describe the look on his face. Before we had a chance to begin our talk, the door burst open, pinning me behind it, and a student shrieked, "Man in the bathroom!" Both men shot out of the bathroom with me staggering behind them. They finally gasped that they must see my records. Upon being told that the records were at my home, they heaved a sigh of relief and agreed to meet me there.

My home was no better than the Tole House. Children were running everywhere; telephones were ringing and so was the doorbell. I seated the men at the kitchen table and gave them my records. They needed more light, so I pulled a lamp across the room, leaving the cord stretched across the doorway. At that moment my poodle, Arpege, ran into the kitchen, coughed twice, and vomited on one man's shoes. He stared in horrified amazement, gagging, as I tried to clean his shoes. The final blow came when the children raced into the kitchen, hit the lamp cord, and brought the lamp crashing down. Both men beat a hasty retreat to the front porch, where they weakly explained to me that I must account for the fact that I paid no sales tax for the month of August. The answer was simple: the Tole House was closed during the month of August, and I had no sales. When I asked them if they understood, they said: "Yes, Mrs. Hauser, we understand. But we don't know if the State of Oklahoma will." I've never been bothered by any tax men since.

In the beginning my business was a total fiasco, but it was a happy and wonderful time. I couldn't afford to hire help, so I traded lessons for help from various students. In exchange for a three-hour lesson each student worked half a day. It was a riot. Each girl who worked in the shop had her own ideas of the most attractive way to arrange the merchandise, and it was moved constantly. We couldn't find anything! The customers took it all with great good nature, and we made it. More important, we had fun doing it. Jerry and the children handled the shipping from our garage, so it really was a family venture.

Students were coming from surrounding towns and even from out of state for painting classes. Many of these people wanted not only to learn to paint but also to learn my teaching methods and techniques. After much careful thought I decided that I would enjoy training teachers, and the Priscilla

Hauser National Tole Teachers Seminar School came into being. Eventually a second small house was purchased for seminar headquarters.

Today there are hundreds of Priscilla Hauser Accredited Teachers around the world, and literally thousands of students have passed through the doors of the seminar house. (A Priscilla Hauser Accredited Teacher is one who has studied the basics of tole and decorative painting with me or with members of my National Teaching Staff for at least 100 hours. The list grows with each tole and decorative-painting seminar that we teach. The teachers are listed at the back of this book.)

In 1970 I was working day and night at the Tole House, and it came as quite a jolt when I discovered that our fourth child was on the way. In the early years Jerry and I bundled the little ones in sleeping bags and took them to the Tole House so we could restock the shelves and take care of the other things that had to be done at night when there were no classes. It wasn't easy, and now we would have to cope with a little one again.

I was quite ill with that pregnancy and was forced to slow down a bit. When one of my students suggested that I should write a book about my teaching methods, I said: "Why on earth would I want to do that? I'm too busy here at the Tole House." She replied, "Just think about it, and remember, if you ever need my help, I'd like to type it for you." As my activities became more limited, her words kept coming back to me. So one day I called Marynell Snow and said, "Marynell, do you really think I could write a book?" She said: "Of course you can. There's nothing to it." Thus Priscilla Hauser Publications began. Marynell is now the editor of all my publications. The first book that I wrote was about dimensional glass painting. It sold and sold well.

Decorative painting became increasingly popular, and I felt that all people who love this hobby should unite. In October 1972 I asked all the teachers, shop owners, and seminar students I could think of to come to Tulsa for a meeting. At that meeting I founded the National Society for Tole and Decorative Painters. Today this organization has well over 8,000 members, with chapters all over the United States.

Marynell encouraged a second book and then a third. With the help of another dear friend who believed in what I was doing, money was provided to help my company grow. Priscilla Hauser Products began to appear on the market. Jerry and the children were delighted. My mother and father were so pleased with the sale of all the books that they were absolutely beside themselves. Without the support of students and family the growth of my tole and decorative-painting enterprises would not have been possible.

Today, some twenty-six books later, the dream of my life has come true with the publishing of this hardcover book. I ask you to join hands with me through its pages and to give tole and decorative painting a try. I promise that the joy it brings to you will be unending.

Introduction to Tole and Decorative Painting

Why should you learn to paint? Well, if for no other reason, for the pleasure it will bring you—and it will bring you pleasure. All it takes is desire; talent truly is not necessary. My method-painting program for tole and decorative painting was developed to teach beautiful techniques, literally step by step, and to make painting as easy as possible. Tole painting actually means the painting or decoration of tinware, but today we call it tole and decorative painting, which means the painting or decoration of any surface, be it wood, glass, tin, or whatever. In decorative painting a pattern is used, and painting is done by a method, a step-by-step technique. Tole and decorative painting is extremely popular because it *can* be learned by anyone who will take the time to read my instructions carefully, study the worksheets, and practice. Believe me, you will learn to paint, and you will love it. Supplies for tole and decorative painting are readily available at craft shops all over the world, and the number of teachers is growing steadily. You can now study right in your own home with the Priscilla Hauser Tole and Decorative Painting Television Workshop, which is currently on cable television from coast to coast.

Now take your paintbrush in hand. Look at it. Study it, work it back and forth in the palm of your hand. Pretend that the brush is a pencil; you're going to learn to use that brush just as you learned to use a pencil. Take control of your brush—don't let it take control of you. Always make yourself as comfortable as you possibly can when you begin to paint. I've always been told that you should sit in a straight chair with both feet flat on the floor, holding the brush as if it were a pencil and you were about to write a letter. This is something I never do. I sit on one foot, with my other leg propped up on another chair. I *do* hold my brush as I hold a pencil—but the most important thing is to be comfortable.

Hold your work so you can turn it as you paint; keep it in the easiest and most comfortable position to paint in and, above all, have fun.

Read and study every page of this book carefully. Read it again and again, because each time you read it, I honestly believe you'll gain a little more from it, and it will all become easier for you to do. Just relax and enjoy your painting.

TERMINOLOGY

Please take the time to read through this section, even though I do not expect you to grasp the full meaning of these terms until you put the techniques into practice. Most of them are taught in detail in the chapter on fundamentals, but reading through this section and familiarizing yourself with the basics will help you as you study.

Paint consistency refers to the thinness or thickness of the paint. It describes the way the paint feels when you mix it with turpentine or some other medium using a palette knife. Proper paint consistency is vital to good technique.

Round red-sable tole brushes are referred to as stroke brushes. They are more graceful than flat brushes, and basic brushstrokes made with them are an important part of good painting technique. Round brushes are not used for drybrush blending or for patting. As you can see in Figure 2-1, the bristles in one of the round brushes are longer than in the other brush. Either brush is perfect for tole and decorative painting, but a beginner may find the short-bristled brush a bit easier to handle. I designed it with this in mind.

The liner brush is a long-haired, round red-sable brush that is used for fine lines, scrolls, and detail. It is sometimes called a scroll brush (Figure 2-2).

Flat red-sable tole brushes are used for strokework, primarily for blending. Many different effects can be achieved with the flat brush (Figure 2-3).

Oil paints are pigments ground in oil. They dry slowly and can be blended beautifully. Some colors are opaque; others are transparent.

Transparent simply means that light can pass through.

Opaque means that light will not pass through.

Acrylic paints are water-based; they dry quickly, but blending is limited by the fast drying time.

Colorbook painting is filling in a solid area between pattern lines with one color.

Outlining is done with a round brush with a fine point or with a liner brush. Fill the brush heavily with thin paint, twist to a point, then outline, using a light touch. Using a light touch means applying as little pressure to the brush as you possibly can.

Double loading means to carry two colors side by side on the brush.

Dirty brush is sometimes used in double loading. A color is used on one side of the brush, with the dirty brush on the other side. To do this, simply fill the brush with paint, wipe the paint out of the brush, and load only one side of the brush with color.

When you double-load a brush with two colors, you must blend *in the same spot on the palette* so that the two colors will blend softly together in the middle. Figure 2-4 shows the difference between a stroke correctly blended on the palette and one in which the color is not softened by blending.

Blending or drybrush blending is the combining of two or more colors. Blending is done with flat red sable brushes. Do not dip the brush in turp while blending: wipe it often on a rag. Light pressure is usually used on the brush.

2-1.

2-4.

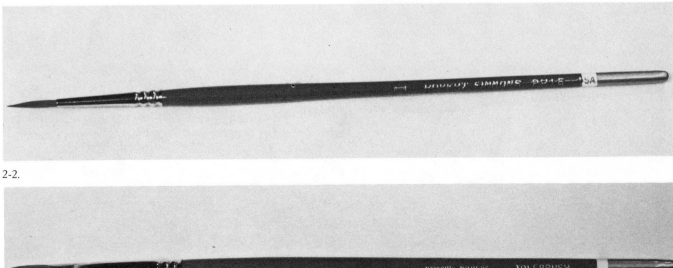

2-2.

2-3.

2-5. Lemons undercoated in white brushing acrylic.

WRONG:

DARK RED   RED   DARK RED

2-6.

DARK RED   RED   ORANGE

RIGHT:
(DARK RED - TO RED - TO ORANGE
CREATES CONTRAST)

Cross-blending describes the brushstroke direction used to pull color from one side of the subject being painted across to the other side.

Pat blending and streak blending are done with the flat red sable brush. A light touch keeps your brushstrokes from showing.

Overblending mixes all the colors that you have applied into one solid color. It can be caused by applying too much pressure on the brush or simply by blending too long. The most difficult part of blending is learning when to stop. This comes with practice. When the subject that you are blending looks good to you, stop. You want to be aware of all the colors that you have applied.

Shading is the use of light and dark colors to create effects of depth and dimension.

Tinting or rouging is a form of drybrush blending. After you have painted and blended a subject, a peach, for instance, you may want to add more pink to it. Do this by picking up a bit of the desired color on your brush and gently patting it on the desired area while the paint is wet.

To paint something that is light in color over a dark background, you may sometimes need to undercoat before painting the subject. For instance, before painting yellow lemons on a black background, undercoat the lemons carefully and neatly with a thin, smooth coat of Priscilla Hauser (ph) white brushing acrylic base coat. Let it dry thoroughly, then paint the lemons. The lemons will appear light and vivid because of the undercoating beneath them. I do not believe in undercoating unless it is absolutely necessary. You must stay exactly within the pattern lines and the paint must be perfectly smooth, or it will show through the finished painting. It is much better to learn to blend with a light touch so that undercoating is not necessary.

Contrast is the key to beautiful painting. It involves sharp differences between two or more colors used on the same subject. Contrast makes your painting look alive, not dull. If you learn to paint with contrast, your work will have zip and sparkle. It will have light and life. Contrast is beautiful (Figure 2-6)!

SUPPLIES

Before we get into the specific supplies that you will need, I want to caution you to always use care and common sense in using and storing these products. *Never* put turp in a glass: it looks like water. Always *read* and *heed* the instructions for *any* product. And for heaven's sake keep all painting supplies out of the reach of children and pets. Our dog once ate an entire tube of white oil paint. Fortunately, it didn't seem to make him sick, but the poor thing pooped white for a week!

Paints

Tole and decorative painting can be done with either oils or acrylics. The finished effect will be different due to the characteristics of the chosen medium. There are advantages to both: acrylics dry much faster; oils allow more blending. I have used acrylics very successfully, but I still prefer oils. Try painting the same pattern with both oils and acrylics. You will enjoy the variety of effects that you can achieve. If acrylics are your choice and you are satisfied with the results, by all means use them.

There are many fine paints on the market today, each with its own characteristics. My favorite brand is Shiva, but try different brands to see for yourself. Look for (1), coverage (opacity), (2) brilliance, and (3) consistency.

When you open a tube of paint and squeeze it from the tube, a great deal of oil sometimes comes out on your palette. This does not necessarily mean that the paint is bad. Oil-pigment separation can be caused by hot or cold temperatures; some pigments just do not mix as readily with oil as others do. If the *paint* is thin and runny as it comes from the tube, then it should be returned to the manufacturer.

Oil paints are fun to buy and use. Many colors are available, and it's great to experiment with as many different colors as you desire. Let me suggest some basic colors that, with proper usage, can achieve almost any color effect you wish (the letters "T" and "O" indicate which colors are transparent and which are opaque):

titanium white (O)
cadmium yellow light (O)
cadmium yellow medium (O)
cadmium orange (O)
yellow ochre (O)
Prussian blue (T)
raw sienna (T)
burnt sienna (O)
raw umber (T)
burnt umber (O)
Shiva cadmium red scarlet (O)
Shiva red crimson (O)
Shiva yellow citron (O)
cadmium red pale (O)
Shiva ferrous black (O)
brilliant yellow light (O)
Shiva leaf green (O)
Shiva violet deep (O)
Shiva ice blue (O)
sap green (T)
asphaltum (T)
olive green (T)

The Priscilla Hauser Beginning Tole Set, manufactured by Shiva, contains twelve colors in small tubes and is excellent for the beginner.

Brushes

Use only the finest red sable brushes, because your brush is your most important tool: your work will only be as good as your brush. I'll agree to skimping on almost any supplies except your brushes. There are many types of brushes available. I have designed and developed my ph tole brushes especially for tole and decorative painting. Robert Simmons, Inc., manufactures these excellent brushes. They have short handles and are made from the finest red-sable or kolinsky-squirrel hair.

You will need both flat and round red-sable brushes. If you are just beginning to paint, I recommend a #4 and #8 PH10 flat red-sable tole brush, a #3 PH20 round red-sable tole or watercolor brush, and a #1 PH15 liner brush. You should eventually get at least every other size from #00 through #16 of flat brush and #1, #3, and #5 round brushes. I use the #1 liner for striping, fine-line, and detail work, and the ph spotting brush for tiny strawberry seeds and faces.

Other supplies are:

ph tracing-paper disposable palette (this serves two needs, since it is both a disposable palette and a pad of tracing paper— I have tried using virtually every surface as a palette and find that mixing paint to the proper consistency, filling the brush, and double loading are more easily done on a tracing-paper palette—do not use a wax-coated palette pad)

palette knife with a flat blade

Shiva Signa-Turp or other odorless turpentine

white and colored chalk

white and gray graphite carbon

paper towels or rags

small jar for turp

ph brush creme and a small bar of Ivory soap for cleaning your brushes

copal medium (optional)

I'd like to explain the use of copal medium at this point. It enables you to thin tube oil colors without diminishing the

2-7.

opacity of the paint. A very small amount of paint thinned with copal will cover adequately and give a very smooth look to your painting. Since copal medium does make the paint slick, patting and blending are more difficult until you learn to use a light touch. I do not recommend it for beginners, but experienced painters will enjoy it.

There are many brands of copal medium on the market. At the present time I am using Taubes copal medium lightweight. If you use copal medium, mix it into all your colors—not just one. Sometimes I fill a small jar lid with copal medium, then dip my brush into it and then into my colors as I paint. Copal dries much faster than turp and will get sticky and tacky on the palette. When this happens, you may add more copal or thin with turp.

Copal medium is a paint extender, so you use less paint, but you cannot save your oils by placing them in the freezer, as you can if turp is used as a medium. Copal palettes do not keep.

Copal can get too old to use. If it is left exposed to air, it can become too tacky to use. If oils mixed with copal are not used within one day, particles of dried paint will form and make a mess of what you are trying to paint.

Brushes must be cleaned with extreme care after using them in copal medium, or they will be ruined. Always dispose of any turp that you have used while painting with copal.

Always clean your brushes after you have finished painting for the day. If proper care is taken, brushes will last quite a long time. To clean a brush, stroke it gently back and forth in a jar of turp. Never abuse or break the bristles. After wash-

ing the brush well in turp place a dab of ph brush creme in the palm of your hand. As you work the brush back and forth in the brush creme, you will see the paint come out of the brush. Rinse the brush in turp again and stroke it gently back and forth on a bar of Ivory soap. Leave the soap in the brush and shape it with your fingers until every hair is in place. This serves as sizing and helps keep the brush in good condition. Soap will not harm brush, turp, or paint. Before using the brush again gently rinse it in turp—*unless* the brush is to be used for dry-brush blending. In that event just flip the dry soap out of the brush with your fingers.

If you wish, eliminate the soap and leave the brush creme in the brush. Be sure to remove the creme from the brush with turp before using. Which way is best? I use both methods.

TRANSFERRING THE PATTERN

Use tracing paper and a fine-point marking pen or pencil to make a careful tracing of the pattern. You may transfer the pattern with graphite carbon or by chalking the back of the tracing. I prefer using chalk, because the lines can always be removed after an item is painted. Graphite-carbon lines sometimes show and are almost impossible to remove.

Let's talk about transferring with chalk first. If the item to be decorated is a medium to a dark color, use white chalk on the back of your tracing. If the background is white or a light color, use brown chalk. On the back side of the tracing go over the lines of the pattern firmly with chalk. Never rub chalk all over the back of the pattern. Shake off the excess dust. Center the pattern on the item to be painted, secure it with

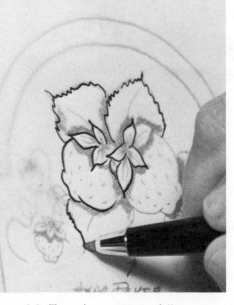

2-8. Trace the pattern carefully.

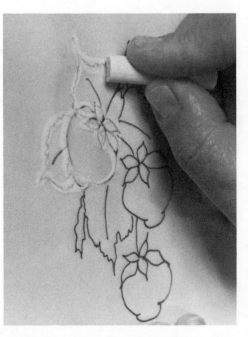

2-9. Chalk the lines on the back of the traced pattern.

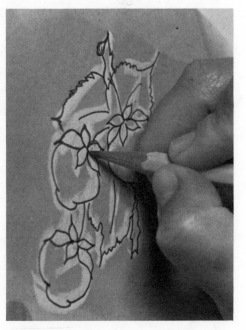

2-10. Go over the tracing lines with light pressure.

masking tape if you wish, and go over the pattern lines with a sharp-pointed pencil or stylus. Do not press hard with the pencil: you do not want to make an indentation on the surface below.

To transfer with graphite carbon, use white graphite on dark surfaces and black graphite on light backgrounds. Position the pattern on the item to be decorated and secure it with masking tape if you wish. Slip the carbon under the pattern and transfer the pattern, using light pressure on the pencil or stylus. Graphite carbon can usually be removed with turp when you are sure that your painting is completely dry. Ink-work is very difficult to do over graphite, since the carbon repels the ink.

2-11. Transferred pattern.

Fundamentals of Tole and Decorative Painting

This is the most important chapter in this book, because the basics taught in it are the foundation for good tole and decorative painting. Please, please read and understand them. Your painting success is based on them. It is possible to paint without knowing these fundamentals, but your work will never achieve the quality and beauty that it *could* have. If you wish to prove this point, read only this first paragraph, turn to the daisy lesson, and paint the very best daisy you can. Then come back and really *learn* and *practice* everything taught in this chapter. When you understand and can carry out the step-by-step instructions in this chapter, paint a second daisy. You will find your painting greatly improved, and your daisy will truly be lovely. The actual learning and practicing is a fascinating experience that will give you a skill you'll enjoy for the rest of your life! Please try. Your best efforts, combined with the painting techniques that I can teach you, are all you need to become an accomplished decorative painter. And remember, anything worthwhile takes a little time, practice, and patience.

PAINT CONSISTENCY

Proper consistency of the paint is one of the most important fundamentals. Consistency refers to the thickness or thinness of the paint. If you add a lot of turp to your paint, the consistency will be very thin. With less turp the paint will be thicker. The consistency should be different for different techniques. The paint must have a thick, creamy consistency for blending; it must be very thin for brushstroke or line-work. Some colors come out of the tube very thick; others may be thin and oily, depending on the pigmentation in the paint. The following descriptions show you how the paint should feel and look when you mix it with turp or another medium. Before you begin to paint, you should always consider: "What consistency should my paint be in order to achieve the best results?"

1. Whipped cream—paint mixed with turp and whipped up and down with the palette knife so that it will hold peaks but still feel soft, not stiff, to the touch. Use this for daisy, rose, and violet petals.

3-1. Whipped-cream consistency.

2. Thin—the paint should be as thin as ink so that it will flow from the brush just as ink flows from a pen. Add many drops of turp. This is the proper consistency for fine lines, curlicues, and striping.

3. Thick creamy—add very little turp. Paint should move easily when it is mixed with a palette knife but be thick and creamy, almost like soft butter. This is the consistency for drybrush blending.

4. Thin creamy—add more turp than for the thick-creamy consistency. The paint should have the consistency of mustard—thin enough to flow from the brush when you are doing strokework.

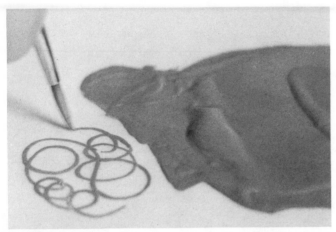

3-2. Thin as ink.

3-3. Thick-creamy consistency.

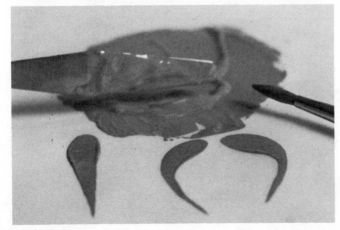

3-4. Thin-creamy consistency.

Always remember to check the consistency of your paint while you are using it. Even though the consistency may be perfect when you first set up your palette, the turp or other medium can evaporate, and, before you know it, the paint can become too thick. If this happens, beware—you'll have a real mess! The few seconds that you spend correcting this will really pay off for you. Your paint *must* be kept at the proper consistency for the technique that you are using.

LET'S BEGIN

There are two main partners involved in good tole and decorative painting: (1) basic brushstrokes with both the flat and round brush and (2) blending techniques. These partners, working together, achieve truly fine decorative painting.

Please follow my directions carefully, especially in the beginning. The way you learn in the beginning will make or break the more advanced techniques you will learn later. Tole and decorative painting can be learned. It is a technique, not a talent. I promise you that, with patience and practice, you can achieve thrilling results. And furthermore, you'll love it!

Practice is necessary, but you can practice too much. I never let my students practice on tracing paper or wax paper more than a few times. They must paint an actual project, and the sooner, the better! So what if it isn't perfect? You're learning, not perfecting. You have plenty of time to develop and perfect after you have learned "how to." If you do not like the work on your first projects, donate them to bazaars or garage sales. You will be surprised and delighted to see that someone else will like them and buy them. And each time you paint something, you will improve. I still have many of my first pieces. They're really bad, but I love them.

BASIC BRUSHSTROKES
The Round Brush

Don't ever let anyone tell you that knowledge of brushstrokes is not important to you as a decorative painter. That is sheer nonsense. Brushstrokes are vital to the total technique. Painting without them is almost like trying to sign your name without an alphabet. In tole and decorative painting your brush is more important than any other painting tool. Buy the best brushes you can and keep them in excellent condition. Without good brushes you will not paint good brushstrokes—and if your paint is not a good *thin-creamy* consistency, forget it! The consistency must be right so that the paint will flow from the brush. Many people try to paint with too thick paint. Don't be one of those people!

Always practice a few brushstrokes with the flat and the round brush each time you sit down to paint. Practice will greatly reward you; painting a few brushstrokes will also help you relax.

There are three basic round-brush strokes that must be learned. These strokes are universal. They are called by many different names, but the strokes are basically the same. These beautiful, basic strokes are easily recognized in the folk-art designs of all countries of the world:

1. polliwog, sometimes called a teardrop stroke
2. polliwog comma angled to the left, sometimes called an eyebrow stroke
3. polliwog comma angled to the right

The #3 ph round red-sable tole or watercolor brush is very versatile. It comes to a very fine point or, if pressure is applied, spreads widely apart. This brush holds a great deal of paint if it is loaded or filled properly.

To paint a polliwog, fill the brush with paint, stroking back and forth in the paint. (The paint should have a thin-creamy consistency and flow smoothly from the brush.) Touch the brush to your tracing paper, apply pressure to the brush, and start lifting and dragging, watching the hairs of the brush—turning (not twisting) the brush *slightly* to the left or right and lifting until a point is formed.

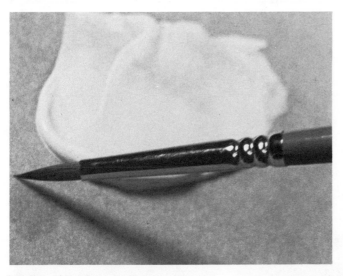

3-5. Round brush at a point.

3-6. Pressure on round brush.

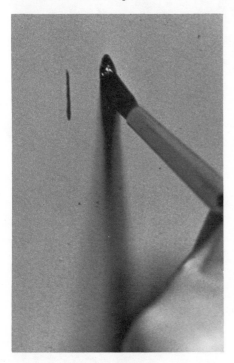

3-7. Touch and apply pressure.

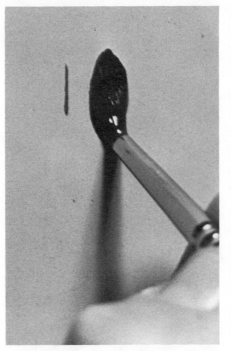

3-8. Start lifting and dragging.

3-9. Finished stroke.

Here are some helpful tips:

1. The stroke should look almost like an exclamation point.

2. Be sure the paint is thin enough to flow easily from the brush.

3. If your hand shakes, don't let it bother you. It will steady with practice.

4. Avoid the common mistakes shown in the illustrations.

5. Practice painting on top of the illustrations. Lay a sheet of tracing paper over the worksheet and make your strokes right over mine. Practice all the strokes on the worksheet (Figure C-1) as often as you feel like it. This will be a big help to you.

To paint a polliwog comma angled to the left, angle the point of your brush toward the left corner of your practice sheet. Touch and apply pressure. Start *lifting* and *dragging*, leaning to the *inside edge* of your brush. Lift until a point is

formed. Polliwog commas are sometimes called eyebrow strokes. They will probably be easier for you to paint than the straight polliwog stroke.

The polliwog comma angled to the right is simply the reverse of the preceding stroke. Angle the point of your brush toward the right corner of your practice sheet. Touch, apply pressure, and start lifting and dragging, leading to the *inside edge* of your brush. Lift until a point is formed.

Do not twist or turn the brush for the comma strokes: just lean to the inside edge of the brush, lift, and drag until a point is formed. It is easier for a right-handed person to paint a comma stroke angled to the left, and for left-handed people to paint comma strokes angled to the right. Practice painting comma strokes in different sizes. I know that this will seem difficult to you at first, but, if you will only have patience, believe me, you *will* learn, and you will be delighted!

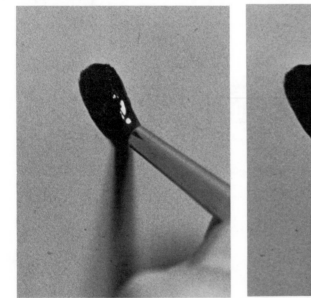

3-10. Touch and apply pressure.

3-11. Start lifting and dragging.

3-12. Finished stroke.

3-13. Touch and apply pressure.

3-14. Start lifting and leaning.

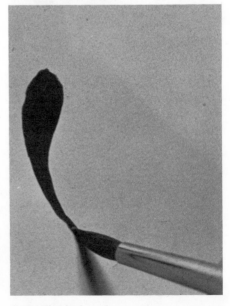

3-15. Finished stroke.

18

3-16.

The Liner Brush

Linework is not really stroke work but the painting of fine, hairlike lines. Linework should be practiced at the very beginning of your learning experience. It will probably take several months of practice to paint fine lines as well as you'd like, but, if you spend a few moments on this exercise each time you paint, before you know it, you will be an expert!

Paint for linework should have a thin consistency. Use a #1 ph liner or the point of a good round red-sable brush. To do linework:

1. Fill the brush completely by brushing back and forth in the thinned paint.

2. Carefully twist the brush in the paint until it forms a fine point.

3. Using a light touch, pull the point of the brush toward you, painting a fine, hairlike line. This is called striping, and good striping takes practice. My hand shakes when I stripe, but I ignore it and do my best. After all, I don't want my work to look like a decal—I want it to look hand-painted!

4. Try making a scroll with the brush.

5. In doing linework always keep your brush full of thin paint. If the paint does not flow smoothly from the point of the brush, thin the paint with a little more turp. Think of the liner brush as a pen. The thin paint must flow from the hairs of the brush just as freely as ink flows from the point of a pen.

3-18.

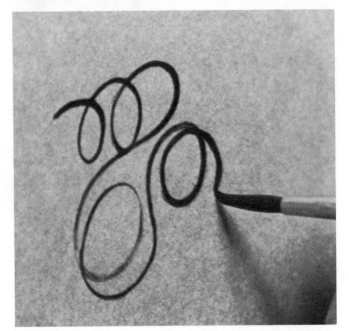

3-19.

3-17.

The Flat Brush

Before you begin to paint the strokes, you must understand the different parts of the flat brush. Study the illustration. To use the flat brush:

1. Use burnt umber or leaf green paint to practice. Thin the paint with turp to the consistency of thin cream.

2. Fill the brush with paint.

3. For the basic stroke touch on the flat edge, apply pressure to the flat surface of the brush, and pull. Easy? Sure!

4. For the line stroke stand the brush on the flat edge and pull, applying almost *no* pressure to the brush. In painting a line stroke the handle of the brush points straight up.

5. To paint a right-side-up half-circle, stand the brush on the flat edge. Apply pressure on the flat surface, hold the pressure, and pivot the brush in your fingers to form a half-circle.

6. For an upside-down half-circle reverse the technique described above.

7. A comma stroke to the left is painted by standing the brush on the flat edge, applying pressure to the flat surface, lifting back up on the flat edge, and pulling.

8. To paint a comma stroke to the right, reverse the technique described above.

9. The S stroke is fun to paint. Stand the brush on the flat edge, pull, apply pressure, lift back up on the flat edge, and drag. To paint really graceful S strokes, you must keep your arm moving toward you as you paint.

In the beginning these strokes may seem a little awkward, but grace and confidence will come with practice. First practice the strokes by placing a sheet of tracing paper over my worksheet (Figure C-1). Fill your brush with paint thinned to the proper consistency and paint your strokes right over mine. You will find that this is the next-best thing to my actually being there with you, taking your hand and guiding you stroke by stroke. As you proceed through the lessons in this book, always remember to make a few practice brushstrokes each time you paint.

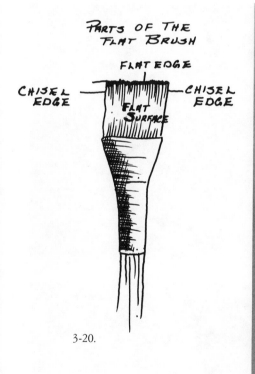

3-20.

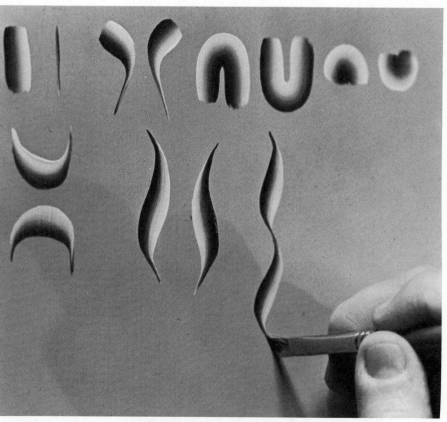

3-21. Basic stroke, line stroke, comma strokes, half-circle strokes, U strokes, and S strokes.

DOUBLE LOADING

To double-load a brush means to carry two colors on one brush at the same time. The colors are not mixed together: one color is on one side of the brush, and the second color is on the other side of the brush. Both flat and round brushes are double-loaded in the same way. You will find that the flat brush is much easier to double-load than the round brush, because the hairs of the former are already spread: the brush does not come to a point.

Practice double loading a flat brush as illustrated on the worksheet (Figure C-1). Read through my instructions completely, then place a sheet of tracing paper over the worksheet and paint your strokes over mine. Do this many times, because double loading is absolutely vital to beautiful painting techniques. It takes time to learn, but keep trying. You *will* get it!

Some people feel that it isn't important to double-load a brush. They just lay down one color, place another color next to it, and blend the two together. This may appear to work at first, but the really beautiful shading that results from a single stroke can never be achieved in this way. Another interesting fact about double loading is that a person who can double-load a brush and shade beautifully with it will in time develop a much faster painting ability than one who cannot.

I once had a student who became so frustrated by trying to double-load a brush that she telephoned me to say that she was not coming to class any more; she had decided to give up. I knew that this student needed her painting desperately, told her it would just take time to learn, and urged her to practice. She kept talking to me, extremely discouraged, when all at once she shouted: "I've done it! I've double-loaded my brush! Wait a minute and let me try it again." She had in fact double-loaded her brush for the first time. She was relaxing while talking to me, not paying any attention to the doodling that she was doing with her paintbrush, so she did a good job of double-loading her brush.

The point I'm trying to get across to you is to *relax*. Don't be uptight about your painting. You may need to try some things such as double loading many times, but success will come if you just let it. If your brush gets messed up, don't despair. Clean the brush in turp, blot it on a rag, and start again.

Dirty brush *is* sometimes used in double loading. A color is used on one side of the brush, with the dirty brush on the other side. To do this, simply fill the brush with paint, wipe the paint out of the brush, and load only one side of the brush with color. This is explained fully in the lesson on double loading.

Good practice colors for double loading are burnt umber and titanium white. These two colors must be thinned with turp to a thin-creamy consistency. Remember to check your paint for proper consistency as you paint. After the paint has been thinned, move the colors with your palette knife to a clean place on your tracing-paper palette. Each puddle should show a nice even edge (Figure 3-24). Study the worksheet (Figure C-1).

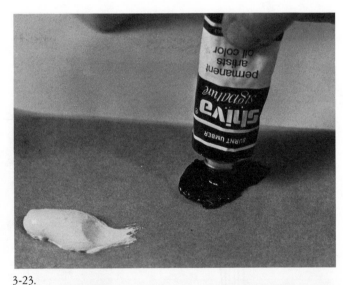

3-23.

3-22. Comma strokes with a double-loaded round brush.

3-24.

The next step is to pick up the brush, put pressure on it, and drag many, many times against the edge of the lighter color. Hold the pressure as you drag. Move to the dark puddle of paint and drag the other side of the brush many, many times against the edge of the paint, putting pressure on the brush.

Many people think that the brush is properly double-loaded and full of paint at this point, but it is not full of paint at all. To properly double-load and fill the brush, it is extremely important and necessary to blend first on one side of the brush, using the same spot on the palette, and then to turn the brush over and blend on the other side of the brush. This forces the paint all the way through the brush from front to back. Each hair will be saturated with paint. It is important to do your blending in the same place on your palette, because this allows most of the paint to remain in the brush while the colors softly blend together. You do not want a harsh division of colors in a double-loaded brush.

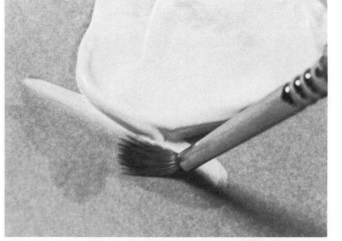

3-25.

3-26.

3-27.

After you have blended on both the front and the back of the brush, go back and pick up more paint on both sides of the brush. At this point the brush will be properly double-loaded. You want the brush to be as full of thin-creamy paint as possible so that you can do a great deal of painting before you run out of paint and have to reload.

Compare filling a brush with paint to washing your hair. The first time that you put shampoo on your hair and wet it, you do not get a whole lot of lather. When that shampoo is rinsed out and more is applied, you get all kinds of lather. The hair in your brush is truly the hair of an animal and must be completely saturated with paint in order to hold that paint properly.

As you paint with the double-loaded brush, the paint may begin to feel a little dry. You can touch your turp with the double-loaded brush, blot it on a rag, and continue painting. This will not disturb the double-loaded brush in any way.

Another point to remember is that double loading a brush can make your palette very messy. There will be places where you have blended on the palette, places where you have moved the paint around, and paint smears where you have stroked up against the puddle of paint. Do take the time to move the paint to a clean spot on the palette. If you do not do this, you will only frustrate yourself and make your painting much more difficult.

3-28.

3-29. If you mess up your brush, clean it in turp and try again. You'll get it!

3-30. Double-loading the round brush is the same except that you must apply constant pressure on the brush to keep the hairs spread apart.

BLENDING

The second basic skill in tole and decorative painting is drybrush blending. Drybrush blending is exactly what the term implies: blending with a dry brush. You do not use a clean dry brush, however: there must always be paint in the brush for drybrush blending. Never touch a perfectly clean brush to the object to be blended: it will just pick up the paint. Always fill the brush with paint, wipe the brush thoroughly, then begin to blend.

Blending is done with the flat red-sable tole brush, using paint with a thick-creamy consistency. If the paint is too thin, it is easy to overblend the colors. You must learn to develop a light touch. When I first began to paint, I tended to be very heavy-handed, because I go at everything in a hard way. Here is an exercise that helped me develop a light touch; I hope it will help you (Figure 3-31).

The photograph shows a rectangular blending exercise. If you are right-handed, place your left arm in front of you and rest your right hand on top of it. If you are left-handed, reverse the procedure. Begin the blending exercise. You can actually feel yourself putting physical pressure on your left arm. Lighten your touch. You must learn not to bear down too hard while blending. This results in overblending and in loss of contrast, which is so important to your painting.

Drybrush blending may be divided into two categories: stroking and patting. Let's talk about stroke blending first. You may stroke-blend from the top of an object to the bottom or from the bottom to the top. Wipe the brush often and use a light touch. The number of times that you should wipe the brush depends on the amount and consistency of the paint that you have applied. It is very important to re-

3-32. Apply color. Paint should be a thick-creamy consistency.

3-33. Stroke-blend from top to bottom. Wipe the brush often.

3-31.

3-34. Wipe the brush. Blend from bottom to top.

25

member not to dip the brush in turp. Drybrush blending is done with a dry brush! I often hold a tissue or soft rag in my hand and wipe the brush by gently pinching the hairs between the tissue or rag. This helps keep every hair of the brush in place while you are blending.

You may also drybrush-blend by stroking from one side of an object to the other. You can pull dark color across to the light, and light color across to the dark. This is called cross-blending. Rarely is anything left in the cross-blended stage. Always go back and gently stroke-blend up and down, following the contour of the object.

The second type of blending is called patting; it is a more advanced form. Patting is done on the flat surface of the flat brush. Use a very light touch to gently move the color. Streaking is a form of pat blending. When you streak, again use the flat surface of the brush, moving the color up and down in little streaks rather like small tornadoes. You can blend dark colors over light or, if you use a *very* light touch, light over dark. Streaks form the wrinkles and folds in fabric. They make poppy and sunflower petals ripple. They form the lines and ridges in green onions and cucumbers. They do so many things! The time that you spend learning patting and streaking is indeed time well spent.

Practice until you have really learned the basic brushstrokes with the flat brush and the round brush, until you have really learned double loading, until you have really learned to blend by stroking, patting, and streaking. Once you know all these techniques, you can apply them to any design with delightful results.

3-35. Cross-blend from right to left or from left to right. Wipe the brush often. Finish blending, following the natural lines of the object. Please use a light touch.

3-36. *Lightly* pat the paint, using the flat surface of the flat brush. Gentle patting will remove the streaks and, if a light touch is used, blend the paint beautifully.

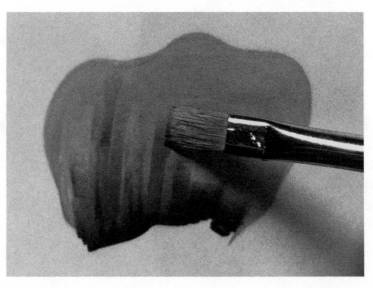

3-37. Streaking.

CONTRAST

In all your painting you must remember to paint with contrast. Strive for contrast *within* the objects as well as contrast *between* different objects in your pattern. Contrast within an object is obtained by shading—painting light and dark areas within an object. In my class Beginning Tole and Decorative Painting I tell my students to keep the dark to the left and the light to the right. This form of contrast within an object is relatively easy to achieve.

Contrast between objects can also be achieved easily if you keep in mind the fact that the parts of a design grow lighter as they come forward. The parts of a pattern that are to the back should be the very darkest; those in the middle area should have a middle or medium value, and those to the front of the design should be the lightest. Of course, an object that is underneath another should be darker than the one that is on top. It will help you to number the objects. Number those to the back #1; use more dark colors in them. Number the middle objects #2 and paint them in medium shades. The #3 objects are in the front and thus call for your lightest colors.

Just remember that the good Lord did not create any two things completely alike; we should not try to paint them alike. Let your work live—let it be full of light and life. Paint with *contrast!*

To conclude this chapter on the fundamentals of tole and decorative painting, let me tell you about a wonderful application. Beautiful Pennsylvania Dutch folk art can easily be done using the two basics of tole and decorative painting: basic brushstrokes and blending techniques. On the worksheet (Figure C-1) you will see a simple heart form, a ball-flower form, and a tulip form. I have combined basic brush-strokes with a flat brush and dry brush-blending techniques to create these three forms. Have fun experimenting with Pennsylvania Dutch patterns. Pennsylvania Dutch design is fascinating in that it lends itself to very old-style decor as well as to abstract and contemporary decor. The few Pennsylvania Dutch patterns that I have included for your painting pleasure are charming exercises for brushstrokes as well as for blending.

To paint the heart, the flat brush was double-loaded with cadmium red pale and Shiva red crimson. A form of the S stroke was used to block in the heart. The right side of the heart was done with a double-loaded brush of cadmium red pale and cadmium orange; cadmium red pale was added to the middle of the heart, and the heart was lightly blended. Feel free to add more dark or light color as needed.

To paint the ball-flower form; apply cadmium yellow medium, burnt sienna, and cadmium orange as shown on the worksheet and blend. The comma strokes around the ball flower may be made with the flat brush or the round brush. I use the round brush.

For the lovely blue shade of the tulip I mixed equal amounts of burnt umber and Prussian blue. The center was filled with brilliant yellow light, and a double-loaded brush with the blue mixture on one side and brilliant yellow light on the other was used to paint the S-type stroke on either side of the tulip. I then wiped my brush and blended carefully, keeping the center of the tulip light. Cross-hatching may be done while the tulip is wet, but it may be easier for a beginner to paint after the tulip is dry. I used my dark blue mixture and a liner brush loaded with very thin paint for the linework.

Preparation of Wood, Tin, and Metalware

Have you ever seen a beautifully decorated piece of wood or metal whose background has cracked or peeled? This happens because of improper preparation at the beginning. Techniques for preparing and finishing items to be decorated are just as important as the techniques for tole and decorative painting themselves.

WOOD

First let's discuss new wood. Woods come in varying degrees of hardness. For example, if you press your thumbnail into a piece of cherry or walnut, it will not make an indentation easily. These woods are very hard. If you do the same thing with a piece of basswood or red cedar, however, an indentation will be made easily because these woods are very soft. Chances are that you will not work much with walnut or cherry. They are beautiful woods but very expensive. White pine is most commonly used for tole and decorative painting. It is not a hardwood, but neither is it very soft. It comes in different grades, depending on the number of knots that it contains. I personally prefer a cheaper grade of pine, as I find knots attractive in most cases. Of course, there are times when a knot might interfere with the subject to be painted, so this must be taken into consideration. White pine will take any type of wood stain or paint, and it antiques beautifully.

There are two ways in which wood can be prepared for tole and decorative painting: staining and painting. If you prefer a stained finish, stain the wood first, then seal it. If you prefer a painted finish, seal the wood first, then paint it. Wood must be sealed because it is porous: the softer the wood, the more porous it is. A wood sealer seals the wood so that paint or any other finish cannot soak in.

After wood has been sealed and the sealer has dried, the wood grain "lifts" to the surface and must be sanded down until it is smooth. Try wet-or-dry Tri-M-Ite paper for sanding. It is available at craft shops and hardware stores. The higher the number on the paper, the finer the grit; the lower the number, the coarser the paper. I use #500 to sand a sealed wooden surface. Tri-M-Ite makes sanding so easy that you won't believe it and, when it is used wet on a sealed surface, eliminates sanding dust. To do this, moisten the Tri-M-Ite paper with tap water. Be sure to sand with the grain of the wood, then dry the wooden object with a rag. *Never wet-sand an unsealed piece of wood:* the water could soak in and damage it. Very hard woods do not require sealing, but, if you are in doubt, go ahead and seal it. For tole and decorative painting white pine, basswood, cedar, and plywood should be sealed; walnut, oak, and cherry may be used without sealing.

If old wood has been painted or varnished and the old finish is not loose, simply sand until smooth, seal with clear acrylic spray, and apply two coats of acrylic-base-coat color. Seal the base coat, antique if desired, and decorate. If the old finish is rough and coming off, you can use a commercial paint-and-varnish remover, but be very careful to follow the instructions and heed the warnings on the container. If the item is a piece of furniture, you would be wise to have the old finish removed by a professional. After the finish is removed, sand until smooth, seal with wood sealer, then apply two coats of acrylic base coat and reseal with clear acrylic spray. Old wood can also be stained, but, in order to do this, every bit of the old finish must be removed, or the stain cannot penetrate.

STAINING

A stain finish requires three steps: staining, sealing, and

sanding. Any good commercial stain may be used, and many lovely colors are available. I enjoy staining with tube oil colors and turp. I save my dirty turp and store it in a can: this old turp works beautifully for staining.

You can stain with any oil color or combination of colors that you desire. To make dirty green, for example, use three parts cadmium yellow medium and one part black or two parts Shiva leaf green plus one part burnt umber. Use straight burnt umber for a deep, dark "brown" stain; raw umber for a "gray" brown stain. Use asphaltum for a gorgeous rich old-pine stain. Burnt sienna is a very reddish brown. A touch of it may be added to a stain, but it is too red to be used alone.

Follow these easy steps for a stained finish:

1. Dip a rag in clean or dirty turp and wipe it over the wood. This slightly seals the wood and helps you stain evenly.

2. Squeeze the desired colors onto a paper palette or wax paper.

3. Rub the turped rag in the colors, then rub the oils onto the board. For a lighter color use more turp; for a darker color use more paint. Be sure to stain the back of the board to give the project a really finished effect.

4. Using clean rags or paper towels, rub the board down. If the board is too light, stain again, using more color. If it is too dark, dip a clean rag in clean turp and rub like mad to lighten the stain.

5. I like to go a step further and redarken the edges of my boards. This adds an almost antiqued look and makes the center of the board appear lighter, which in turn accents the finished decorative painting. To darken the edges, apply a small amount of burnt umber all the way around the top or outer edge of the board. Using a circular motion, rub the umber into the wood with your finger. Blend this darkened edge into the rest of the stain by rubbing in a circular motion with a dry rag or paper towel. Blend gently, working from the light area into the dark edges. Be sure to leave the edges dark—but do not let the dark area look like a ring around the light area. You must have a soft, gentle blend from light to dark.

6. If you have stained with tube oils and turp, apply a thin, even coat of ph wood sealer over the wet oil stain. The sealer will be dry enough to sand in approximately two hours. If other products are used, let the stain dry, then seal the project. Sand the dry sealer lightly. Touch up with paint or stain if needed.

Note: The amount of time required for any paint product to dry depends a great deal on the weather. Humidity is an extremely important factor. If the weather is dry and hot, drying will go well; if the day is humid, you must allow more drying time. A blow hair dryer is a good thing to have around when you're trying to dry a sealed board in a hurry. Turn the hair dryer on the sealed board for just a few minutes: this will speed the drying considerably.

4-1. Apply burnt umber to the edges of the board.

4-2. Rub umber into the board, using your finger.

4-3. Blending with a circular motion.

PAINTING

In preparing a wooden project for tole and decorative painting, never use a high-gloss enamel. The slickness of a high-gloss finish makes decorative painting extremely difficult, since the oils tend to slide. This enamel also chips easily. Use a semigloss or satin-finish enamel, either brush-on or spray, or ph brushing acrylic base coat. If you use spray paint, both the paint and the item to be spray-painted should be at room temperature. Always shake the can very thoroughly. Some pigments take longer to mix than others. I like to spray into a box so that the excess paint is confined to a small area. Use a number of light coats rather than one or two heavy coats: this helps to avoid runs in the paint. If the paint does run, quickly wipe it off, then carefully start building up paint in that area until the overall depth of the color is obtained. When you have finished painting, always turn the can upside down and spray until no more paint comes out. Wipe the nozzle before putting the can away. Remember, too, that a clogged nozzle can be replaced by your paint dealer.

In my opinion the simplest and loveliest finishes for base-coating wood are my ph brushing acrylics. They come in lovely rich colors and are available in small jars. Before applying the base coat be sure to shake the jar vigorously to mix the paint. I like to use a sponge brush to apply the brushing acrylic and usually use two coats, allowing 30 minutes drying time between coats. After the last coat let dry 30 minutes, then spray the painted board with two or three light coats of ph clear acrylic spray. This is not always necessary, but some base-coat colors are more porous than others. Since blending is easier on a sealed surface, it is a good idea to seal the base coat with clear acrylic spray. If antiquing is desired, it may be done after the acrylic spray is completely dry. Sometimes I antique an object before decorating it; sometimes I decorate it, then antique the whole thing. This depends entirely on the effect that you want to achieve.

While we are on the subject of wood finishes, I want to tell you about my ph tole finish. This excellent product was designed especially for tole and decorative painting. As you know, oils tend to dull considerably as they dry. The ph tole finish brings the color back to life with an intensity and depth, giving added richness to painted projects. The tole finish can be applied as soon as the oil paints feel dry to the touch, because the finish actually breathes, allowing the paints to complete the drying process. Drying can take weeks and in some cases even months.

This beautiful satin finish is quick-drying and easy to use. It comes in both brush-on and spray forms. The brush-on tole finish can be applied with either a bristle or a sponge brush. Drying time is 1 to 1½ hours, depending on the humidity, and two coats will usually suffice. Bristle brushes may be cleaned in turp. If you use a sponge brush, simply wrap it in foil and store it in the freezer. It can be used for

several more applications of tole finish before you throw it away.

Although tole finish is primarily for tole and decorative painting, it also works beautifully for découpage. Since it does dry quickly, several coats can be applied in the same day. It really is a beautiful finishing touch!

ANTIQUING

There are many good antiquing glazes on the market. My ph antiquing glaze is clear: no oil color is added to it. By using a small portion of clear glaze and adding any combination of oil colors to it you can create outstanding color combinations that are not available in any store. To do this, stir the glaze thoroughly, then spoon out approximately ⅛ cup into a throwaway container. To this add about ½ teaspoon of one or more oil colors. For a dirty green color use ¼ teaspoon burnt umber and ¼ teaspoon leaf green or olive green. For a rich brown use ¼ teaspoon burnt umber or asphaltum and ¼ teaspoon raw umber. A very dark antiquing glaze is made with ¼ teaspoon burnt umber and ¼ teaspoon black. A lovely blue can be created with ¼ teaspoon Prussian blue and ¼ teaspoon black.

Mix the tube oil paint and the ph antiquing glaze together. Brush the glaze on the object to be antiqued. Using a folded, soft rag, begin wiping off the antiquing glaze. Continue until the desired effect is achieved. If you remove too much of the glaze, simply apply more and wipe again.

TIN AND METALWARE

The first thing that I do for old tin pieces is to make a thin paste of any dishwasher detergent and water, cover the item with this paste, and let it set for about 30 minutes. By the way, do wear rubber gloves: dishwasher detergent can take the skin right off your hands. Using a steel-wool pad, scrub the metal, rinse in water, and dry thoroughly. To remove rust and to prevent its recurrence, I recommend Rusticide, or naval jelly, which is available at most hardware or paint stores. Wipe Rusticide on metalware with a rag. If there is no rust on the item, apply Rusticide as a preventive measure. Let the Rusticide dry overnight or until it no longer feels oily to the touch. In addition to removing and preventing rust this product also etches the metalware so that the base coat of paint will adhere to it properly. As a rule I spray-paint metalware. I do not like the brushstrokes to show. Spray with several light coats of paint until the item is completely covered, let dry, antique if desired, and the metalware is ready for tole and decorative painting.

My base-coat acrylics may also be used on metalware. Use a small, fine piece of sponge to pat the paint onto the metal. This gives a lovely, smooth effect. Seal the base coat with clear spray, antique if desired, and decorate.

Note: If you have a good marked piece of old metalware, do not cover the identifying mark with paint. Obliterating such a mark will detract from the value of the metalware.

Preparation of new tin and metalware is short and sweet. It should be wiped with Rusticide, allowed to dry, base-painted, and decorated.

TWO-COLOR BACKGROUNDS

You can give a very lovely and professional look to many items by using a combination of either two colors of paint or—on wood—a combination of stain and paint. To combine stain and paint, first stain the wood, let dry, seal, let dry again, and sand. Transfer the oval or pattern of your choice to the wood and paint the oval with two coats of brushing acrylic. Let dry, then spray two or three times with ph clear acrylic spray. Carefully stripe the wooden item if desired. (Masking tape may be used if needed to help keep lines straight.) Transfer the pattern and paint the design.

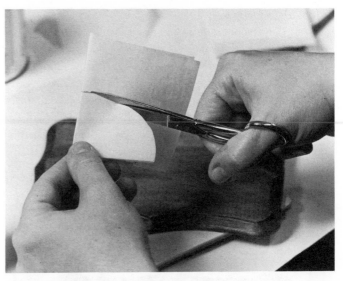

4-6. Fold paper into fourths and cut out an oval.

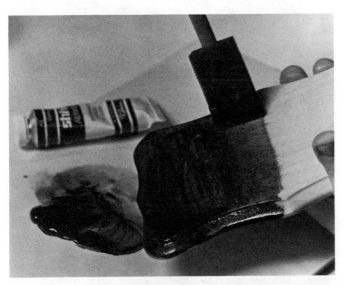

4-4. Stain the board with burnt umber and turp.

4-7. Position the paper oval and draw around it with chalk.

4-5. Seal the board. When it is dry, sand lightly.

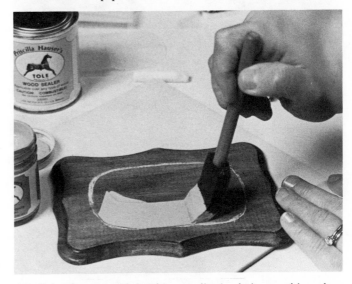

4-8. Paint the oval with brushing acrylic. Apply it smoothly and evenly.

FINGER STRIPING

You can give your projects an extra touch by adding a stripe of color around the edges or on various portions of the object you are decorating. To add a finger stripe, simply dip your finger lightly into brushing acrylic, then draw it carefully and smoothly along the line where you wish to place the color. The amount of pressure that you apply will determine the width of the finger stripe. If you make a mistake, don't be alarmed. Just remove that part of the stripe with a damp cloth, wipe dry, and resume striping.

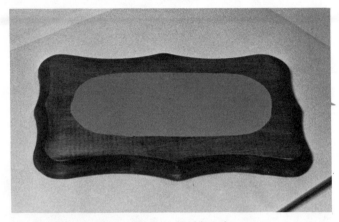

4-9. Brushing-acrylic oval on a stained board.

4-11. If you want a two-tone effect with antiquing glaze, draw an oval on contact paper.

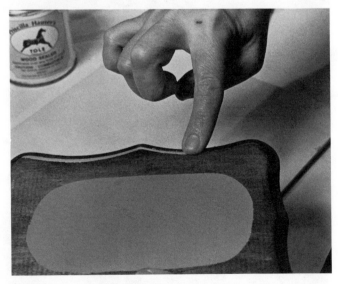

4-10. Finger striping adds a nice touch.

4-12. Fold the paper into fourths and cut out the oval.

4-13. Press the contact paper into place, making sure that the edges stick securely.

4-15. Wipe off the excess glaze.

4-14. Apply antiquing glaze to the entire surface, including contact paper.

4-16. Remove the contact paper. Touch up the edges of the oval if needed.

Leaves

Leaves are one subject that all of us must learn to paint. In tole and decorative painting you will find leaves not only with all flowers and fruits but, as you advance, in the bouquet of daisies that the dear little girl you are painting is holding. If you are painting owls or eagles, they are probably sitting on a branch, and there are *leaves* on the branch. So get with it from the start: promise me that you will practice painting leaves whenever you have a chance. You will soon develop an enjoyable technique.

There are three types of leaves that you should learn to paint. The first leaf, which I teach to all my beginners, is the basic leaf. It is the simplest leaf to paint. Even though you will learn a more advanced and more attractive leaf later, there may be times when you are in a hurry and want to use the basic leaf. The second leaf is called the basic brush-stroke dry brush-blend leaf. The general form of this leaf can be applied to almost any type of leaf that you desire to paint. Learn to paint the Basic Leaf first, and, when you feel you have mastered it fairly well, begin to practice the second leaf. The techniques for these leaves are shown step-by-step on the color worksheet (Figure C-2). Study them carefully, then place a sheet of tracing paper over them and paint with me, stroke by stroke. With practice and patience you will learn to paint beautiful leaves, and you will enjoy doing it! The third leaf that you should learn is the turned leaf, which adds so much to any design, especially one that contains a lot of leaves. This leaf is so valuable to the decorative painter that I have included a separate color worksheet (Figure C-3) for it. Practice it, following my instructions. You will love painting these beautiful leaves.

THE BASIC LEAF

One leaf by itself is not a particularly beautiful thing, but many well-painted leaves can combine to create lovely borders and even complete designs. Leaves serve as a frame for fruits and flowers, and no two leaves are exactly the same.

In the beginning and intermediate levels of decorative painting we do not work with an established light source. We're painting designs on trays and around milk cans rather than painting a still-life design where the light is coming from one direction. Just remember to paint the leaves to the back of the design very dark; the leaves in the middle of the design should be a medium value, and the leaves to the front—or on top—a very light value. Sometimes it helps to number the leaves in the pattern. Let the #1 leaves be the dark ones, the ones to the back of the design. Let the #2 leaves be the medium value, the leaves to the middle. The leaves to the front of the design, which are the lightest, will be the #3 leaves.

Now, to help you paint dark, medium, and light leaves, I want you to mix three shades of leaf green as shown on the color worksheet (Figure C-2). To mix the dark, or #1-value, leaf green, mix a little ferrous black into Shiva leaf green until a *very* dark green is reached. (By the way, if you can't get Shiva leaf green, you can mix it by adding just a little of any black to cadmium yellow medium.) For the #2 middle-value leaves use Shiva leaf green or the mixture of black and yellow described above. For the #3 lightest leaves mix equal amounts of Shiva leaf green, Shiva yellow citron, and titanium white or brilliant yellow light. By using these three shades of leaf green you will be able to get beautiful contrast between the dark, medium, and light leaves.

Additional colors that may be blended into the #1 dark leaves are more burnt umber, burnt sienna, raw umber, and even a little ice blue. Now, I realize that ice blue is light, but it truly gives the dark leaves depth and beauty—don't be afraid to try it. For the #2 leaves you may blend in any medium-value color, such as cadmium yellow medium, Shiva yellow citron, or even a little cadmium orange. For the #3 lightest leaves you may blend in any light-value color, such as brilliant yellow light and/or titanium white, ice blue, or sometimes even a little cadmium yellow light.

As a general rule of thumb, paint your leaves with the base, or bottom, of the leaf toward you, placing the darkest shading color you are using on the left side of the leaf and the lightest shading color on the right side of the leaf. We use this rule of "dark to the left, light to the right" until much later in decorative painting when we work with an established light source.

I hope you have read and somewhat understood what I have said so far about painting leaves. I also hope you have studied the leaf worksheet (Figure C-2), as it will help you learn very easily. Now, the only way to really get the job of learning done is to practice and practice the basic leaf. The following instructions will take you through the painting of a #2 medium-value leaf. The #1 and #3 leaves are painted exactly the same way: you simply adjust the colors for the value of leaf you are painting.

Study the color worksheet (Figure C-2) carefully. Look at the contrast between leaves. It is important that you learn to include contrast *within* each leaf and contrast *between* the leaves. To paint the practice leaf on the worksheet, use a #4 ph flat red-sable tole brush and a #1 ph liner brush. The size of the brush depends, of course, on the size of the pattern.

1. Thin the paint to a thick-creamy consistency.

2. Double-load the flat brush with leaf green on one side and a touch of burnt umber on the other. Blend on the palette to soften the color.

3. Paint the left (dark) side of the leaf first. Remember that you are doing decorative—not realistic—painting. In your first year do not worry about establishing a light source. It's hard enough to learn to paint without having to worry about where the light is coming from. Touch the brush at the bottom of the leaf; paint two strokes as illustrated. Pick up more green and umber and refill the brush. Touch at the bottom of the leaf, apply pressure to the brush, hold the pressure, and pull, lifting up on the flat edge of the brush at the top point of the leaf. You may paint from the base of the leaf up, or, if it is easier for you, turn the leaf around and pull the stroke toward you, lifting up on the flat edge of the brush. Find the position most comfortable for you. It will make your painting easier. The dark area at the base of the leaf represents a shadow. If the base of the leaf does not fall under another object in your pattern, omit the dark shadow.

4. Double-load the brush with leaf green and titanium white. Blend on the palette to soften the color, then paint the right (light) side of the leaf. The white should be to the outside.

5. The two sides of the leaf are blocked in, but there is a hole left in the middle. This is the most fun part of the basic leaf. In that hole you can dab on a little leaf green and always a little yellow. To me yellow is sunshine, and it adds light and life to the leaf. Add a bit of Shiva yellow citron or any other medium-value color you choose. Wipe the brush thoroughly: *don't put it in turp!* Using a light touch, blend the leaf. Study the color worksheet (Figure C-2) carefully.

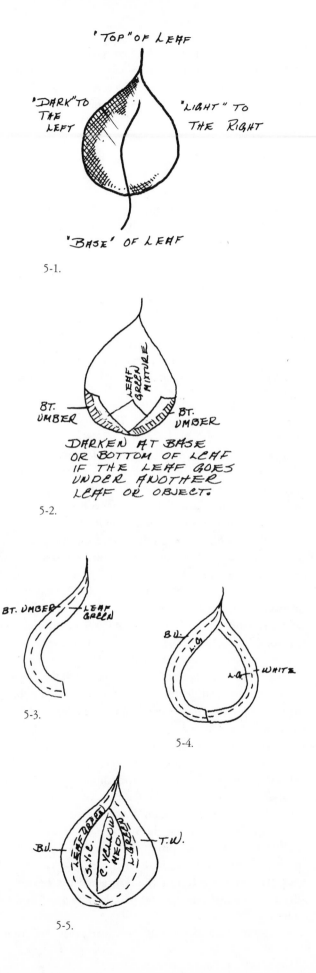

5-1.

5-2.

5-3.

5-4.

5-5.

Here are some helpful tips on perfecting your leaf:

1. Feel free to add a touch of any color you desire to your leaves, as long as you use dark values on dark leaves, medium colors on medium leaves, and light values on your lightest leaves. For example, when I paint strawberries or apples, I blend a tiny touch of red in the leaves; if I am painting roses, I add a bit of the rose color; when I paint blue violets, of course, a touch of blue is blended into the leaves.

2. Be careful not to overblend.

3. Use a light touch. If you apply too much pressure on the brush or blend too long, all the colors will mix together, giving the leaf a solid look. You want to be aware of all the lovely colors that you have applied.

4. As you blend, be sure to wipe the brush often.

A vein is a curved line—never a straight line. It starts at the bottom of the leaf and stops short of the top. It is painted in the darkest shading color, which in this case is burnt umber. The paint must be thinned with turp so that it flows freely from the brush. You can paint the vein with a liner brush, the point of a round brush, or the flat edge of a flat brush. Some beginners find it easier to allow the leaf to dry slightly before painting the vein.

THE BASIC BRUSHSTROKE DRYBRUSH-BLEND LEAF

For this leaf use a #4 ph flat red-sable tole brush and a #1 ph liner brush. Colors are the same as for the basic leaf. For your #1, or darkest, leaves, mix Shiva leaf green with a touch of ferrous black. Other colors to blend into #1 leaves are burnt umber and titanium white or brilliant yellow light. For the #2 medium-value leaves use leaf green; colors to blend into #2 leaves are burnt umber, titanium white or brilliant yellow light, cadmium yellow medium, and Shiva yellow citron. The #3, or lightest, leaves require a mixture of equal parts of leaf green, Shiva yellow citron, and brilliant yellow light. (Color swatches are shown in Figure C-2). Other colors to blend into #3 leaves are burnt umber, brilliant yellow light, and/or ice blue or titanium white.

The following instructions tell you how to paint a #2 medium-value leaf. Paint this leaf with the base (bottom) toward you, keeping the dark color to the left and the light color to the right.

1. Thin the paint to a thick-creamy consistency.

2. Double-load the brush with leaf green and burnt umber. Blend on the palette to soften the color.

3. Paint two S strokes at the base of the leaf as shown. Double-load the brush again, touch on the flat edge of the brush, apply pressure to the flat surface of the brush, and pull in toward the bottom of the leaf. Place a second stroke on top of the first in the same manner.

4. To paint the top of the leaf, stand the brush on the flat edge, umber side up, and pull. Let the brush roll to the left.

5. Double-load the brush with leaf green and titanium white. Blend on the palette to soften the color. Study the illustration of the right and wrong ways to paint this side of the leaf (Figure 5-9), then paint two commalike strokes opposite the strokes on the other side of the leaf. When you paint these two strokes on the right-hand side of the leaf, your wrist will be in a very awkward position.

6. After the leaf is blocked in, there will be a hole in the middle. To fill in this space, dab in the colors of your choice—always medium-value. I usually apply a little leaf green, yellow to add light and life, and Shiva yellow citron.

7. Wipe the brush carefully and begin to blend, using a very light touch. Blend from the base of the leaf out or from the outside edges of the leaf in. Do as much blending as you wish but do not overblend, or you will lose all the lovely colors that you have put into the leaf.

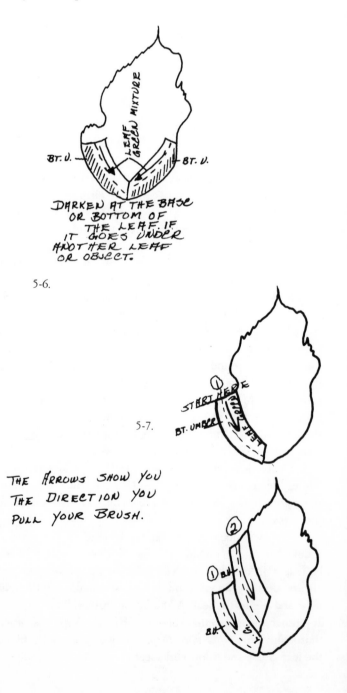

5-6.

5-7.

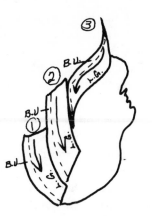

YOUR BRUSH ANGLE WILL BE
PERPENDICULAR ON STROKE
#3

5-8.

Here are some helpful tips for this type of leaf:

1. Do not paint a B on the right-hand side of the leaf. Most beginners do so when painting a leaf for the first time, perhaps because it is very comfortable to angle the brush down to the left when the brush should angle to the right. Using the proper brush angle will help you avoid this common mistake.

2. You may go back over any or all of the strokes as many times as needed to block your leaf in satisfactorily.

3. In painting a leaf stroke from the outside edge in toward the center. Never stroke from the inside of the leaf outward.

4. Work clockwise with your strokes as you block in the leaf.

5. Always remember to work for contrast *within* each leaf and *between* the individual leaves in a design. How dull it would be to paint all leaves the same!

Leaves require a lot of practice, but don't let them stump you. Go ahead and paint your flowers and fruit. In time you will find that your leaf technique improves tremendously.

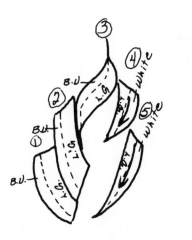

5-9.

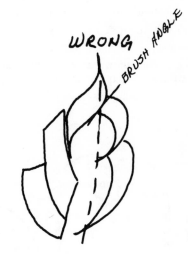

5-10.

TURNED LEAVES

Before you begin to paint a turned leaf, you should study it carefully to understand how it turns. On this leaf (Figure 5-11) the entire upper end is turned over the top of the leaf. If you have studied the basic leaf and the basic brushstroke drybrush-blend leaf, you know that a leaf is painted with the base or bottom toward you, placing the dark color to the left and the light color to the right. The basic brushstroke drybrush-blend leaf should be well understood before attempting turned leaves.

If the entire end of a leaf turns, then one side of the turned edge should technically be dark, and the other side light. This is one way in which it may be painted. The step-by-step photographs will be of great help to you in understanding this turned leaf.

In painting the leaf shown in the color worksheet (Figure C-3), I used a #8 ph flat red-sable tole brush. Of course, the size of the brush depends on the size of the pattern. Use any combination of colors you wish. The following suggestions may be of help to you. Use Shiva leaf green or mix a leaf green with cadmium yellow medium plus a touch of ferrous black. I also used burnt umber, titanium white, Shiva yellow citron, Prussian blue, cadmium orange, and Shiva ice blue. (You can mix ice blue with a touch of Prussian blue, a touch of burnt umber, and a lot of titanium white.) Use yellow citron, ice blue, and cadmium orange as accent colors. All colors should be mixed with turp to a creamy consistency.

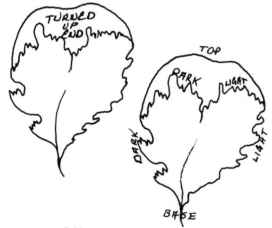

5-11.

1. Double-load a #8 flat brush with leaf green on one side of the brush and burnt umber plus a touch of Prussian blue on the other side. Blend on the palette to soften the color. Paint the first stroke. Remember that your pattern is a guide and *only* a guide. Do not worry about staying within the pattern lines exactly.

2. Place the second stroke on top of the first stroke.

3. Stand the brush on the flat edge. Let the umber edge of the third stroke touch the umber edge of the second stroke. Pull. Apply pressure on the brush as you pull, then lift back up on the flat edge at the center point of the leaf.

4. Double-load the brush with leaf green and titanium white. Blend on the palette to soften the color. Turn the leaf on its side so that the umber edge is on the bottom, or toward you. Stand the brush on the flat edge, pull, apply pressure, and lift back up on the flat edge at the center point of the leaf.

5. Paint the fifth and sixth strokes as illustrated (Figure 5-16).

6. After blocking in the edges of the leaf shadow under the turned end. On the light side shadow dark, using a little burnt umber and just a touch of Prussian blue.

7. On the dark side of the leaf you have several choices. For instance, you can shade in a darker value than the turned edge, using a little more Prussian blue. Technically speaking, it should be darker, since it is the shadow beneath the turn—but, remember, you are doing decorative painting and are not working with an established light source. You can shade lighter, using Shiva yellow citron or another light color. Still another way to shade is to blend the turned (top) section fairly lightly on what would normally be the dark side. In other words, paint the whole turned-over edge relatively light, then paint the dark shadow directly underneath the turned edge. You will find one of these leaves on the color worksheet (Figure C-3). Study it carefully.

8. After the leaf is blocked in and shadows placed as desired, add the colors of your choice to the remaining areas of the leaf. Wipe the brush, pat, and blend. Again, study the color worksheet.

5-12.

5-13.

5-14.

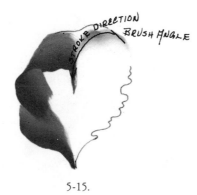

5-15.

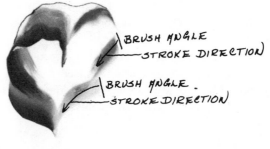

5-16.

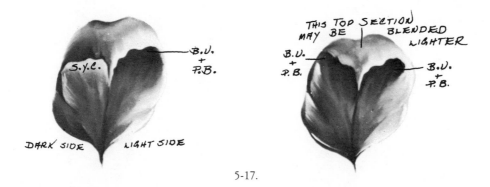

5-17.

A leaf with one turned edge is relatively simple, especially if the turn is on the light side of the leaf. The left, or dark, side of the leaf is blocked in as usual, then three strokes are painted to execute the turn. Follow the instructions, the photographs, and the color worksheet (Figure C-3):

1. Double-load with leaf green on one side and burnt umber plus a touch of Prussian blue on the other. Paint the first stroke.

2. Refill the brush and paint the second stroke.

3. Refill the brush, stand it on the flat edge, dark side up (at the top of the leaf), and paint stroke #3.

4. Double-load with leaf green and titanium white. Paint stroke #4.

5. Refill the brush and paint stroke #5.

6. Refill the brush and paint stroke #6.

7. Apply burnt umber and Prussian blue shadows against the turned edge. Add the colors of your choice to the center. Wipe the brush, pat, and blend. Study the color worksheet and practice!

Confused? I hope not. Read these instructions through several times. Practice by placing a sheet of tracing paper on top of the color worksheet and painting your strokes directly over mine. I know that all the pieces will fall into place for you.

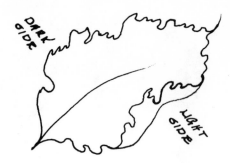

5-18.

5-19.

5-20.

5-21.

5-22.

5-23.

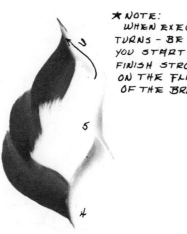

5-24.

★ NOTE:
   WHEN EXECUTING
TURNS — BE SURE
YOU START AND
FINISH STROKES
ON THE FLAT EDGE
OF THE BRUSH

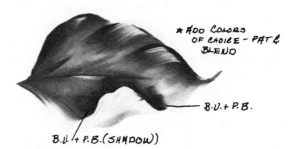

★ ADD COLORS
   OF CHOICE — PAT &
   BLEND

B.U. + P.B.

B.U. + P.B. (SHADOW)

5-25.

Daisies

Daisies are one of the simplest flowers to paint. The petals are actually brushstrokes, which I hope you have been practicing! Daisies exhibit much depth and beauty. There are two types: one is painted with the flat brush, and the other with the round brush. I think that the flat-brush daisy is the prettier of the two, but the round-brush daisy teaches a lot about brush control and stroke technique. Try painting both types of daisies, then decide which works best for you.

For the round-brush daisy use a #3 ph round red-sable tole brush. This is the correct size for painting the practice daisy on the color worksheet (Figure C-4). If the pattern were smaller, you would need a smaller brush, just as a larger pattern would call for a larger brush. For the worksheet flat-brush daisy use a #3 ph flat red-sable tole brush. Again, the size of your brush depends on the size of your pattern. You will also need a #1 ph flat red-sable tole brush for the daisy center and a #1 ph liner brush for linework.

Which colors should you use? The base coat can be any color. The top coat should be titanium white. For a pale green daisy, for example, use a pale green base coat and a titanium white top coat. For white daisies use Paynes gray for the base coat and titanium white for the top coat. For the daisy center use cadmium yellow medium, burnt sienna, burnt umber, titanium white, or cadmium red pale. Thin the base-coat color to a thin consistency, the white to a whipped-cream consistency, and the other colors to a creamy consistency.

All daisy petals are formed with two coats of paint: a base coat, which is always a color, and a top coat of whipped titanium white. The base-coat stroke does not need to be a neat stroke. It should not fill up the pattern completely, and the color should be very soft. Use only a small amount of the base-coat color in your brush, because too much paint would bleed through the white top coat, giving the daisy too much color. In applying the top coat remember that the daisy petals should be graceful strokes, starting at the outside edge of each petal, pulling in toward the center, and lifting neatly to a point at the center of the daisy. Let the strokes flow with the natural curve of the daisy.

BRUSH STROKE DIRECTION

6-1.

Following are some helpful tips for painting daisies:

1. Petals do *not* lift to a point on the back side of the daisy.

2. Be sure that all petals except those on the back *do* lift to a point.

3. Study the pattern to determine the proper spacing between the petals.

This is the technique for painting the daisy center:

1. Using a flat brush, paint the daisy center yellow, but leave a little space for shading down the left side across the bottom, as illustrated (Figure 6-2).

2. Double-load a small, flat brush with cadmium yellow medium and burnt sienna. Blend on the palette to soften the color and, with the burnt sienna on the outside, shade in the empty space down the left side and across the bottom of the daisy center. Wipe the brush, pat, and blend.

Note: In shading a daisy center do not apply the burnt sienna over any yellow color. If you do, the yellow will lighten the burnt sienna, and the daisy center will look washed-out and flat.

If desired, you can paint fine, hairlike lines on each daisy petal. Darken your base-coat color by adding a touch of burnt umber. Thin this darkened color to a thin consistency. Use a liner brush to paint fine, hairlike lines radiating from the center out onto each petal. All lines should flow from the same spot on each petal. The finer the line, the lovelier the finished look will be. It may be easier for you to paint the lines after the daisy petals have dried slightly. Remember—for good linework the paint must have a thin consistency.

To finish the daisy, use the point of the liner brush to apply tiny dots of burnt umber, cadmium yellow medium, titanium white, and cadmium red pale around the outside edges of the daisy center. Let some of these dots actually fall onto the petals.

My choice for the daisy leaf is the basic brushstroke drybrush-blend leaf. Be sure to use a lot of color and contrast in your leaves, keeping those to the back of the design dark and those to the front light. Remember, too, that leaves underneath daisies or other leaves should be shaded darker in the areas where they would be in shadow.

6-2.

6-3.

6-4.

6-5.

Lemons

When you shop in the fruit department of the grocery store, lemons and other citrus fruits are among the least attractive. Apples and pears have beautiful natural shading, but, if lemons are shaded (with burnt umber), that means they're rotten! I take the liberty of adding my own shading and lots of it to lemons, because I am a great believer in contrast and color. I believe that, if you paint with contrast and lots of color, your work will be outstanding.

Use flat brushes: the size of the brush depends on the size of the lemon pattern. For this lesson (Figure C-5) I suggest a #2 and a #7 ph flat red-sable tole brush.

Colors that can be used include: titanium white, cadmium yellow light and/or cadmium yellow medium, raw sienna and/or yellow ochre, cadmium red pale, burnt sienna, and Shiva yellow citron.

This is how to paint the lemon:

1. Undercoat the center of the lemon in titanium white.

2. Wipe the brush and pick up cadmium yellow light. Paint all the way around the white.

3. Wipe the brush and pick up cadmium yellow medium. Paint all around the yellow light.

4. Wipe the brush and pick up raw sienna or yellow ochre. Paint all around the yellow medium.

5. Wipe the brush and double-load with raw sienna and Shiva yellow citron. *Blend on the palette to soften the color.* Shade across the top (the lightest edge) of the lemon. Pick up more paint and go back over this area as many times as you need to. Don't be afraid to use more paint if you feel that you need it.

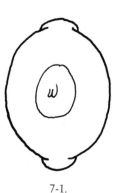

7-1.

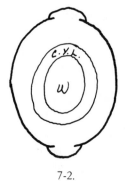

7-2.

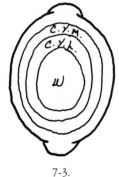

7-3.

THE COLOR SET UP CAN BE SLOPPY. DONT WORRY ABOUT OVERLAPPING COLORS. DONT USE TOO MUCH PAINT.

7-4.

7-5.

6. Wipe the brush and pick up a little cadmium red pale. Add a small amount of this red on the dark side of the lemon as shown (Figure 7-6).

7. Double-load the brush with yellow ochre and burnt sienna. Blend on the palette to soften the color. Shade the dark side of the lemon.

8. Wipe the brush or use a soft, dry brush; pat and blend.

9. Apply colors to the lemon end as shown in the color setup (Figure 7-8). Wipe the small brush and very carefully pat and blend.

Either the basic leaf or the basic brushstroke drybrush-blend leaf may be used for the lemon leaf. Regardless of your choice, remember to *paint with contrast!* You can add interest to your design by turning one or two leaves.

Here are some helpful tips for painting lemons:

1. Try not to let your pattern grow. Stay within the pattern lines. A badly shaped lemon is not attractive!

2. In painting a group of lemons shade those to the back of the design darker; those to the front, lighter. Variation of color is important.

3. Always paint what is on the bottom—or underneath—first, then work up toward the top. Figure 7-9 shows the sequence in which the leaves and lemons should be painted.

4. If you plan to paint lemons on a very dark background such as black, you may want to undercoat them neatly with a thin, smooth coat of white brushing acrylic. This will make the yellow very bright.

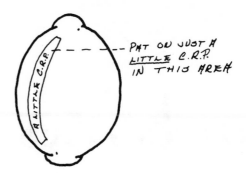

7-6.

7-7.

YOU MAY ADD MORE OF ANY OF THE COLORS IF NEEDED.

REMEMBER — BLENDING IS SLOW — TAKE YOUR TIME.

COLOR SET UP: LEMON ENDS

7-8.

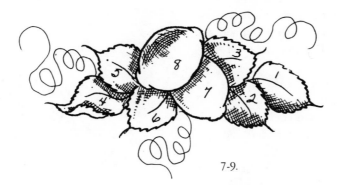

7-9.

Strawberries

Strawberries are almost everyone's favorites. They lend themselves well to designs for kitchen, bathroom, and certainly family room. Strawberries are beautiful with daisies and are not difficult to paint. They do take a little time, but they are definitely worth it.

Use flat brushes: the size of the brush depends on the size of the strawberry to be painted. For this lesson (Figure C-5) use a #1 and a #5 ph flat red-sable tole brush and a #1 liner brush for the strawberry seeds.

Strawberry colors include: titanium white, cadmium red pale, cadmium red scarlet, Shiva red crimson, Shiva yellow citron, cadmium orange and/or cadmium yellow deep, and cadmium yellow light or cadmium yellow medium (optional). I rarely use yellow in my strawberries: to me a yellow strawberry looks old, not fresh, but this is a matter of opinion, and, if you would like to use a touch of yellow in your strawberries, do so.

Here is how to paint a ripe strawberry:

1. Undercoat the center of the strawberry with white oil.

2. Go all the way around the white with cadmium red pale. Go all the way around the cadmium red pale with cadmium red scarlet.

3. Double-load the brush with cadmium red scarlet and Shiva red crimson. Blend on the palette to soften the color. Shade the left (dark) side of the strawberry.

4. Wipe the brush. Double-load with cadmium red scarlet and cadmium orange and/or cadmium yellow deep. Blend on the palette to soften the color. Shade the right (light) side of the strawberry.

5. Wipe the brush and gently pat and blend. Be sure that your strokes flow in the direction in which the strawberry grows. Cross-blend if desired. Be sure that the final blending strokes straighten out so that they follow the contour of the strawberry.

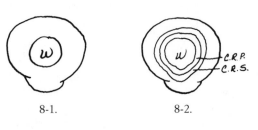

8-1.   8-2.

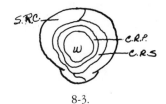

8-3.

8-4.

Strawberry seeds are painted with the point of the liner, and their application can make or break a strawberry. The student often paints too few or too many—or makes them too large or too small. The worksheet (Figure C-5) shows you the correct size. Paint them carefully, using cadmium yellow medium, and don't rush. Each little seed is not a dot but an elongated dot. On the left side of the strawberry the seeds curve to the left; on the right side, to the right. They are straight in the middle of the strawberry. The seeds are outlined on the outside edge with a very, very fine hairlike line of ferrous black. This line of black gives depth to the seeds and actually sets them into the strawberry. Strawberry seeds should always be applied while the strawberry is wet, because they are *in*—not on—the strawberry. When you do linework of any kind, such as these fine, hairlike lines on the outside of the strawberry seeds, your liner brush must be full of paint. The paint must be very thin so that it will flow freely from the point of the brush.

Here is how to paint an unripe strawberry:

1. Undercoat the center of the strawberry with white.

2. Fill in the entire right (light) side of the strawberry with Shiva yellow citron.

3. Add a little cadmium red pale on the left side of the strawberry, then a little cadmium red scarlet.

4. Double-load the brush with cadmium red scarlet and Shiva red crimson. Blend on the palette to soften the color and shade the left (dark) side of the strawberry.

5. Wipe the brush thoroughly and gently pat and blend. A great deal of green should show in the unripe berry.

6. The seeds are applied to the unripe berry in the same manner as for the ripe berry.

If a design includes a lot of small strawberries, I paint them as unripe berries.

Strawberry bracts are painted exactly like tiny basic leaves. Bract colors are leaf green, burnt umber, yellow, and white. Use a #1, #0, or even a #00 ph flat red-sable tole brush. The bracts should be painted after the strawberry has dried, or the red will mix with the bract colors, making them look muddy.

On the color worksheet (Figure C-5) you will see that I have used the basic leaf for the lemon design and the basic brushstroke drybrush-blend leaf for the strawberries. When properly done, both leaves are beautiful—so the choice is yours.

ENLARGED SEEDS

 YELLOW
FINE LINE OF BLACK

ON THE LEFT SIDE OF THE BERRY THE SEEDS SHOULD CURVE TO THE LEFT. ON THE RIGHT SIDE TO THE RIGHT. STRAIGHT IN THE MIDDLE.

8-5.

8-6. 8-7.

8-8. 8-9.

8-10.

Dimensional Apples

RED APPLES

The first time that I ever saw a big red apple painted on a black background, I thought that it was absolutely marvelous and knew that I must learn to paint such real-looking apples. When you first read these instructions, they may sound a little involved, but I know that if you read and study them carefully, then paint an apple three times, you will be amazed and delighted with the results. The more you practice, the better you'll become, and you will find yourself enjoying a whole new experience—the art of tole and decorative painting.

Brushes for apples are #4, #6, #8, and #10 ph flat red-sable tole brushes. Colors are titanium white, cadmium yellow medium, cadmium red pale, cadmium red scarlet, Shiva red crimson, cadmium yellow deep or cadmium orange, Shiva yellow citron, and Prussian blue. Using a few drops of turp on your palette knife, thin each color on your palette to a thick-creamy consistency. Paint *must* be kept at this creamy consistency in order to blend well.

Here is how to paint the red apple (Figure C-6):

1. In your mind picture an imaginary line just below the point of dimension on the apple and do not apply paint above this line until you are so instructed.

2. Using the #6 brush, undercoat the center of the apple with titanium white. Go all the way around the white with cadmium yellow medium, around the yellow with cadmium red pale, and around the cadmium red pale with cadmium red scarlet. Apply Shiva red crimson down the left side and across the bottom and cadmium orange or cadmium yellow deep down the right side of the apple.

3. Use your #10 brush to blend the apple. Be sure that the brush is dry—with no turp on it. As you blend, be sure that your brushstrokes flow in the natural direction in which the apple grows.

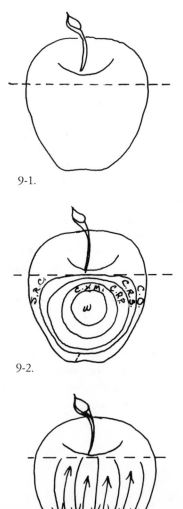

9-1.

9-2.

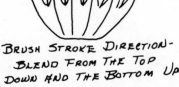

BRUSH STROKE DIRECTION—
BLEND FROM THE TOP
DOWN AND THE BOTTOM UP

9-3.

4. Using the #4 flat brush, apply a big yellow "smile" of cadmium yellow medium directly on the line of dimension. The yellow paint should be fairly thick for this smile. The yellow does not quite touch the edges of the apple on either side. Thoroughly wipe the brush (do not dip it in turp) and pull the yellow smile down into the apple a stroke at a time. Be sure to wipe the brush after each pull. You may add more yellow paint if you desire. Pull the color, then wipe the brush. Be sure that your brushstrokes follow the shape of the apple, as shown (Figure 9-5).

5. Apply a half-circle of yellow just above and just touching the smile.

6. Fill in behind the half-circle with cadmium red scarlet. Apply Shiva red crimson on the left side of the top and cadmium orange on the right side. Wipe your small, flat brush and carefully blend the red colors together. Wipe your brush often.

7. The next step is to pull the cadmium red scarlet down into the yellow. *Brushstroke direction is all-important*, as this is where the dimension is formed. Study the illustration (Figure 9-8) and pull the color accordingly. Wipe the brush after each pull.

8. Wipe the brush. Pick up a little cadmium yellow medium and pull just a bit of it back up in the other direction. Wipe the brush after each stroke. A touch of Shiva yellow citron may be added if desired.

9-6.

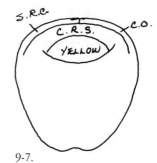

9-7.

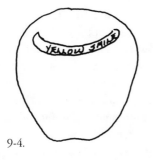

9-4.

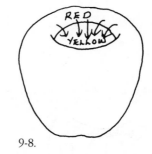

9-8.

9-5.

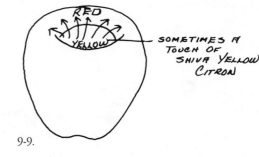

9-9.

9. Add the tiniest touch of Prussian blue in the very throat of the apple and carefully pull it up. This touch of blue gives beautiful depth to the point of dimension.

10. The final step is to pat another smile of Shiva red crimson over the yellow smile. Wipe the brush and pull the red smile down into the apple.

The blossom end of the apple is painted in the same way as the stem end. Of course, the blossom end is smaller.

Here are some helpful tips for painting apples:

1. Do not overblend. You want to be aware of all the colors that you have applied to the apple.

2. Use a light touch in blending. Don't be heavy-handed.

3. In blending turn the project that you are painting around in your hands so that you are as comfortable with it as possible. You may find it easier to pull the brush toward you.

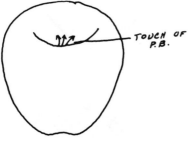

9-10.

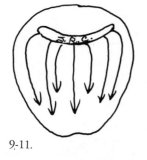

9-11.

9-12.

STEMS

The stem of the apple or of any fruit, for that matter, is a detail. It must be painted carefully and neatly. If you have done a beautiful job of blending your fruit, don't ruin it with sloppy-looking stems. A stem may be painted while the fruit is still wet, or you may wait until it is dry and paint the stem on top of the dry paint. If you choose to add the stem while the fruit is wet, dip your flat brush in turp, blot it on a rag, and clean out the area where the stem is to go.

Stem colors are titanium white and burnt umber. I sometimes use a touch of Prussian blue along with the burnt umber, but a beginner must be very careful in doing this. Ice blue— really, any color desired—can be used in a bark stem.

The size of the brush depends on the size of the stem to be painted. Very small brushes are generally required, such as a #00 or #0 flat tole brush and a #1 liner for detail work.

Using your small, flat brush, apply colors as shown on the color worksheet (Figure C-6). Slide down the outside edge of the stem and pull the dark color across to the light in a curved manner. *Use a light touch.* If you are heavy-handed, you will lose the entire effect of the bark that you are trying to create. Wipe the brush after every stroke if necessary. Pull the light color across to the dark. Add more dark or light if necessary. Notice that there is a dark area all across the stem directly under the cut end. Apply colors to the cut end of the stem as shown on the color worksheet, working carefully and neatly. Blend lightly.

GREEN APPLES

Green apples aren't easy to paint. The reason why they are not as easy to paint as red apples is color. For red apples you use white, red, yellow, brilliant and vibrant cadmium orange, and the very deep, dark Shiva red crimson. Consequently, it is difficult to overblend a red apple. The colors in a green apple simply do not create severe contrast, making overblending very easy. You must be careful and pay attention to what you are doing when you paint the green apple. If you follow my instructions carefully, take your time, and study the color worksheet (Figure C-6), you will be delighted with the results.

This lesson shows you how to paint one green apple step-by-step. Please remember that, in developing a design containing more than one apple, you should vary the colors. Paint the apples to the back of the design much darker than those to the front of the design. Contrast between the apples is vital.

For the apples on the color worksheet I used a #4 or a #6 flat sable tole brush to apply the colors and a #8 or a #10 brush for blending. As always, the size of the brush depends on the size of the apple to be painted.

Apple colors are titanium white, brilliant yellow light, cadmium yellow medium, Shiva leaf green, Prussian blue, burnt sienna, Shiva ice blue, Shiva yellow citron, and sometimes an accent of cadmium orange of cadmium red pale.

Study the apple pattern. In most patterns you will see either a stem end or a blossom end. This forms the point of dimension. Imagine a line just below the point of dimension, as illustrated (Figure 9-13). Do not apply any paint above that imaginary line until you are directed to do so. Here is how to paint the green apple:

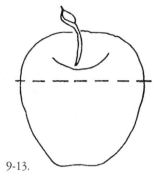

9-13.

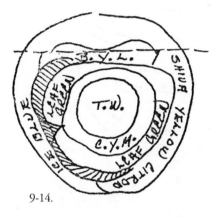

9-14.

1. Using your palette knife and turp or copal medium, cream the paints to a *thick*-creamy consistency.

2. Fill a #4 ph flat red-sable tole brush with titanium white. Apply as illustrated (Figure 9-14).

3. Wipe the brush. Pick up cadmium yellow medium and apply it around the white.

4. Wipe the brush, pick up leaf green, and apply it around the yellow.

5. Wipe the brush. Double-load with leaf green on one side and burnt sienna plus a tiny touch of Prussian blue on the other. Be sure not to use too much Prussian blue and do not mix the burnt sienna and Prussian blue together. The results will not be the same if you do this. Apply the dark shading color around the green.

6. Wipe the brush thoroughly. Double-load with just the dirty brush on one side and ice blue on the other. Apply the ice blue clear out to the edge on the left side of the apple.

7. Wipe the brush. Double-load with leaf green and Shiva yellow citron. Blend on the palette to soften the color. Apply the citron on the right side.

8. Wipe the brush and pick up brilliant yellow light. Apply just below the point of dimension, which is rather like a smile.

9. Fill a #10 brush with titanium white, then wipe the brush thoroughly. Begin to blend, using a light touch, pulling from the point of dimension down toward the bottom and pulling from the bottom of the apple up toward the point of dimension. Be sure to follow the natural curve of the apple. Study the color worksheet (Figure C-6).

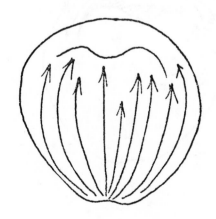

9-15.

10. Wipe the brush and cross-blend either from the left to the right or from right to left (see Figure C-6). Cross-blending moves the color across the apple from one side to the other. You do *not* want the apple to look as if it has an outline of ice blue or yellow citron. You may add more of any color you need, but *you must blend with a light touch.*

11. Wipe the brush and blend back up and down, following the natural curve of the apple. (You cannot leave an apple in the cross-blended stage.)

12. Now you are ready to paint in the point of dimension—the upper portion of the apple where the stem joins the apple or where the blossom end of the apple is located. Using a #6 or smaller dirty brush, wipe the paint out of the brush and double-load with the dirty brush on one side and burnt sienna plus a touch of Prussian blue on the other. Paint an S stroke directly on the smile, or point of dimension, as shown on the color worksheet (Figure C-6). This takes practice!

13. Apply the colors as illustrated (Figure 9-18) above the S stroke. Wipe the brush, gently pat, and blend.

14. If a stem joins the apple, carefully paint the stem to come down into the apple. If the blossom end is visible, paint it neatly and carefully, using a liner brush. Please remember—painting a beautiful stem or blossom end is as important as painting the apple. There is nothing more disheartening to me as a teacher than to see a beautiful apple with a lousy stem or blossom end. *Practice!*

If you desire, a touch of cadmium orange or cadmium red pale may be applied to a small area of your choice on the apple. If you have never painted green apples before, chances are that you will need to paint at least six of them in order to catch on. You can do it, but you must read and follow the instructions carefully.

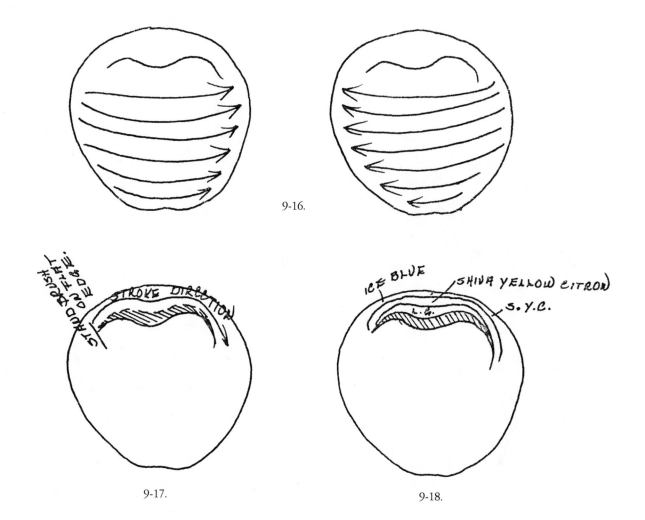

9-16.

9-17.

9-18.

Pears

The pear is one of the most beautiful fruits that you can paint, and I enjoy teaching students to put a great deal of color into it. If you read and follow the directions carefully and thoroughly understand the pear's construction before you begin to paint, I know that you will enjoy painting pears.

Brushes for pears are a #4 and a #8 ph flat red-sable tole brush and a #1 ph liner brush for detail work. For a yellow pear the colors are titanium white and/or brilliant yellow light, cadmium yellow medium, yellow ochre, burnt sienna, cadmium orange, Shiva yellow citron, and sometimes a touch of cadmium red pale or Shiva red crimson. For a green pear the colors are titanium white, cadmium yellow medium, Shiva leaf green (or cadmium yellow medium plus a touch of black), burnt umber, burnt sienna, Prussian blue, and Shiva yellow citron.

Let's look at the way in which a pear is put together. The top part is smaller than the bottom part. Colors are applied to both parts separately; the parts are blended separately; then the two are blended together. The yellow pear is explained in the instructions—the color setup for the green pear is given at the end of the lesson:

1. Thin the paints if necessary to a thick-creamy consistency. Fill a #4 brush with titanium white and undercoat the center of each section of the pear.

2. Wipe the brush and pick up cadmium yellow medium. Paint all the way around the white. Wipe the brush and pick up yellow ochre. Paint all around the yellow in each section.

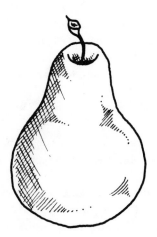

10-1.

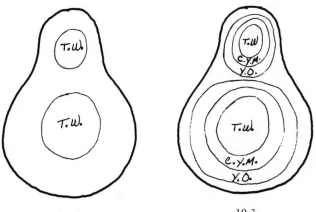

10-2.   10-3.

3. Wipe the brush and double-load with yellow ochre and burnt sienna. Blend on the palette to soften the color. With the burnt sienna to the outside, shade down the entire left (dark) side of the pear.

4. Clean the brush. Double-load with yellow ochre and Shiva yellow citron. Blend on the palette to soften the color. With the Shiva yellow citron to the outside, shade down the entire right (light) side of the pear.

5. A completely dry brush should not be used to blend the pear. Fill the #8 brush with yellow ochre, then wipe it thoroughly. (Never dip the brush in turp unless you are so instructed.) Begin to gently pat and blend the top section of the pear. Add more color if needed. Be careful not to overblend. Brushstroke direction should follow the natural lines of the fruit.

6. Wipe the brush thoroughly and begin to blend the bottom section of the pear. Follow the pear's natural curve as you blend. If needed, cross-blending may be used to pull the dark color across to the light or the light color across to the dark. After the cross-blending is completed, wipe the brush and lightly blend again, following the contour of the fruit.

7. Blend the two sections together. Wipe the #8 brush thoroughly, then gently blend from the top of the pear to the bottom, following the natural curve of the pear and using as light a touch as possible. Refer to the color worksheet (Figure C-7).

8. In blending the two sections together an indentation of dark color is needed on the left side, and an indentation of light color on the right side. This creates dimension. Place this shading where the pear sections join in a figure-3-type shape (Figure 10-10).

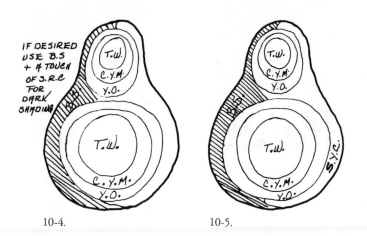

10-4.　　　　　　　10-5.

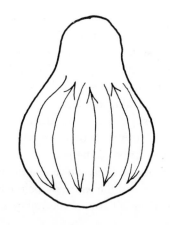

BLEND TOP SECTION

10-6.

BLEND BOTTOM SECTION

10-7.

54

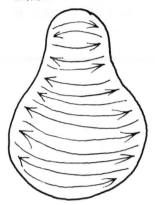

CROSS BLENDING - YOU MAY BLEND FROM DARK TO LIGHT OR LIGHT TO DARK.

10-8.

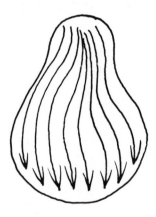

FINISH BLENDING UP AND DOWN - FOLLOWING THE NATURAL DIRECTION THE PEAR GROWS.

10-9.

10-10.

Pears are sometimes blushed or tinted with a touch of color. The technique is almost like applying a touch of rouge to the cheeks—hence the term rouging. The color worksheet (Figure C-7) will help you add this delicate touch to your pear. The color is applied after blending is completed and while the paint is still wet. Use either cadmium red pale or Shiva red crimson. Thoroughly wipe the brush used for blending and pick up a tiny touch of color. Ever so lightly *pat* and blend this color where desired on the pear.

A point of dimension must be painted where the stem meets the pear:

1. Use burnt sienna plus a tiny touch of burnt umber thinned to a thin consistency. Fill the #1 liner brush with this dark color and paint a smile at the top of the pear.

2. Fill a #1 flat brush with burnt umber plus a touch of burnt sienna. Wipe the brush thoroughly, then carefully pull the smile down into the pear. Let the strokes follow the natural lines of the pear as illustrated (Figure 10-12).

SMILE IS - B.S plus A LITTLE B.U.

10-11.

10-12.

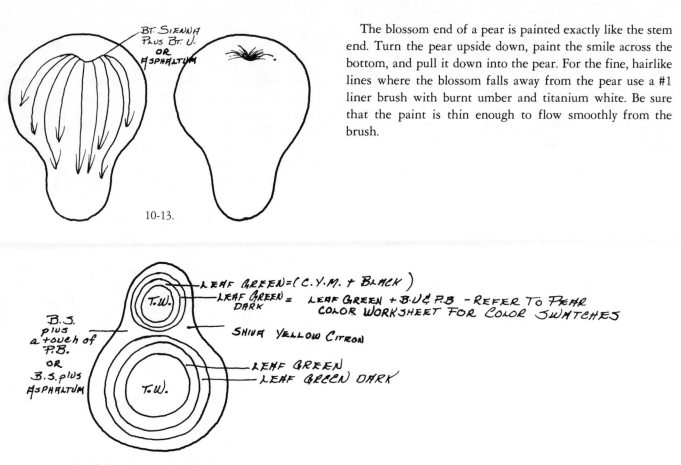

BT. SIENNA
PLUS BT. U.
OR
ASPHALTUM

10-13.

The blossom end of a pear is painted exactly like the stem end. Turn the pear upside down, paint the smile across the bottom, and pull it down into the pear. For the fine, hairlike lines where the blossom falls away from the pear use a #1 liner brush with burnt umber and titanium white. Be sure that the paint is thin enough to flow smoothly from the brush.

LEAF GREEN = (C.Y.M. + BLACK)
LEAF GREEN DARK = LEAF GREEN + B.U & P.B - REFER TO PEAR COLOR WORKSHEET FOR COLOR SWATCHES

B.S. plus a touch of P.B. OR B.S. plus ASPHALTUM

SHIVA YELLOW CITRON

LEAF GREEN
LEAF GREEN DARK

T.W.

T.W.

10-14. Color setup for green pear.

Peaches

Peaches are among the loveliest of fruits. Their coloring can vary from soft yellow tinged with pink and yellow-green to a deep yellow tinged with cadmium red pale and burnt sienna. The many different colors in peaches require long and careful blending but must *not* be overblended.

Brushes used are #4, #6, and #8 ph flat red-sable tole brushes. Colors are titanium white, cadmium yellow light and/or medium, yellow ochre, Shiva yellow citron, Shiva red crimson, burnt sienna, and cadmium orange. Thin the paints with a few drops of turp to a thick-creamy consistency.

Note that a peach is divided into two sections. Apply colors as described, following the color worksheet (Figure C-7):

1. Using a #4 flat brush, undercoat the center of both sections with titanium white.

2. Wipe the brush and pick up cadmium yellow medium. Apply the yellow all the way around the white.

3. Wipe the brush and pick up yellow ochre. Apply it around the cadmium yellow medium.

4. Wipe the brush. Double-load with the dirty brush on one side and cadmium orange on the other. Blend on the palette to soften the color and shade down the right (light) side of the peach with cadmium orange.

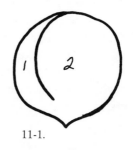

11-1.

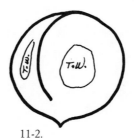

11-2.

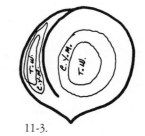

11-3.

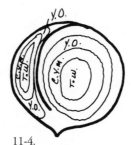

11-4.

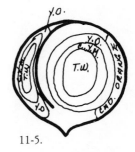

11-5.

5. Wipe the brush and double-load with yellow ochre and Shiva yellow citron. Blend on the palette to soften the color. Apply yellow citron across the bottom of the peach as illustrated (Figure 11-6).

6. Wipe the brush. Double-load with the dirty brush on one side and burnt sienna plus Shiva red crimson on the other. Blend on the palette to soften the color and apply the paint as shown (Figure 11-7).

7. Fill the #8 flat brush with titanium white, wipe it well, and begin to pat and blend. Blend up and down, following the natural lines of the fruit. Cross-blend, then blend back up and down. I like to blend each section of the peach separately, then to carefully pat and blend the two sections together. *A very light touch* is of the utmost importance. It takes a long time to blend a peach. Care must also be taken not to overblend. You need to be aware of all the beautiful colors in the peach. More of any color can be added carefully if needed. Remember, *color contrast* is vital to the beauty of the finished peach.

In a grouping of peaches you want color variation. Peaches to the back of the design should be darker; those closer to the front should be lighter. Vary your colors. Use more yellow in some peaches, more Shiva yellow citron in some, more cadmium orange in others.

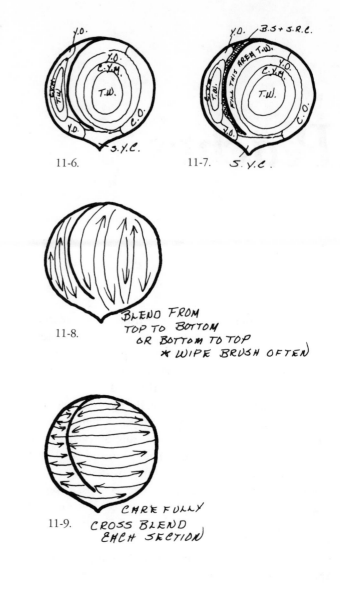

11-6.

11-7. S.Y.C.

11-8. BLEND FROM TOP TO BOTTOM OR BOTTOM TO TOP ★ WIPE BRUSH OFTEN

11-9. CAREFULLY CROSS BLEND EACH SECTION

Mushrooms and Grass

MUSHROOMS

I believe that the mushroom is here to stay. Like the daisy, the mushroom will never grow old to the decorative painter. Painting these interesting little fungi, with their different sizes, colors, and shapes, is intriguing. You may not be aware of the magnificent range of colors found in mushrooms and toadstools—almost any color you can imagine, from hot orange and purple to soft off-white and cream colors. You will find a little study of mushrooms and toadstools most rewarding, particularly in regard to their different shapes and colors.

As you read through this lesson, study the drawings and the color worksheet (Figure C-8). They will enable you to understand the mechanics of painting mushrooms. Once the mechanics are understood, all you need is practice. There are many different techniques for painting mushrooms. The following instructions explain basic techniques—not too easy or too difficult—an intermediate level of decorative painting. Practice these techniques, and later, if you want to study more advanced methods of mushroom painting, you will have no trouble mastering them.

Use flat brushes. The size of the brush depends on the size of the mushroom to be painted and blended. Always use as large a brush as you can handle. For the practice mushrooms use a #1 ph flat red-sable tole brush for the color setup and a #5 ph flat red-sable tole brush for drybrush blending.

For a red mushroom use titanium white, cadmium red pale, cadmium red scarlet, Shiva red crimson, cadmium orange, burnt umber, and burnt sienna. For a pink mushroom use titanium white, Naples yellow or brilliant yellow light, Venetian red, and raw umber. (This combination may not sound too great, but try it: it's beautiful!) For a white mushroom use titanium white, Naples yellow light or brilliant yellow light, raw umber for brown-gray shading, black for blue-gray shading, olive or sap green for a greenish tint, and burnt umber for brown shading. The red mushroom is used as an example in the following lesson. Color setups for the other mushrooms are given on the color worksheet (Figure C-8).

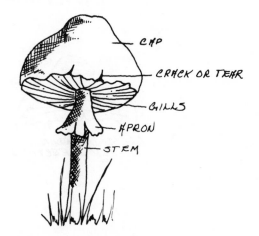

12-1. Parts of a mushroom.

Here is how to paint the mushroom cap:

1. Using a #1 flat brush, undercoat the center of the mushroom with titanium white. Wipe the brush. Pick up cadmium red pale.

2. Go all the way around the white with cadmium red pale. Wipe the brush. Pick up cadmium red scarlet.

3. Go all the way around with cadmium red scarlet.

4. Double-load the brush with cadmium red scarlet and Shiva red crimson. Blend on the palette to soften the color. Shade across the top, down the left (dark) side of the cap, and partway across the bottom.

5. Double-load the brush with Shiva red scarlet and cadmium orange or white. Blend on the palette to soften the color and shade the right (light) side and across the bottom of the mushroom cap.

6. Wipe the brush (do not clean it in turp) and begin to pat and blend. Use as large a brush as you can handle. Blend and wipe, following the natural growth direction of the mushroom. You may blend from top to bottom and/or from bottom to top. *Remember to wipe the brush often and to use light pressure.*

7. If you want to pull the dark and/or light color in from the sides of the mushroom cap, you may cross-blend. Finish blending up and down, following the natural lines of the mushroom cap. More color can be added at any time during blending.

12-2.

12-3.

12-4.

12-5.

12-6.

12-7.

The little cracks or tears in the mushroom cap are not difficult to paint, and they add a great deal to the finished look of the mushroom:

1. Fill a #1 liner or fine-pointed brush with burnt umber of a thin consistency. Paint the cracks.

2. Double-load a #1 or smaller flat brush with Shiva red scarlet and titanium white. Blend on the palette to soften the color. Shade *around* and *right next to* the cracks or tears in the mushroom, placing the white next to the umber crack. Wipe the brush and gently pat and blend. Refer to the color worksheet (Figure C-8).

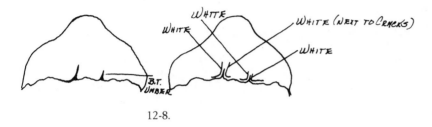

12-8.

Here is how to paint the mushroom gills:

1. Undercoat the gill area in titanium white. Do not go all the way to the outer edges or to the edges of the stem.

2. Double-load a #1 or smaller flat brush with titanium white and burnt umber plus burnt sienna. (Pick up burnt umber, then burnt sienna on the same side of the brush.) Blend on the palette to soften the color. Shade all the way around the outside edges of the gill and the mushroom stem.

3. Wipe the brush thoroughly, then begin to pull and streak the burnt umber from the edge of the stem across the white to the edge of the mushroom gill. *Be sure to wipe your brush each time that you pull the dark across the light.* Follow the brushstroke direction as illustrated (Figure 12-11), then, *if needed*, pull the dark from the outside edge across to the stem edge. *Your brushstroke direction is all-important:* it will either make or break the gill area of the mushroom.

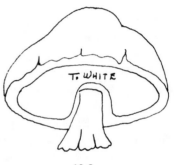

12-9.

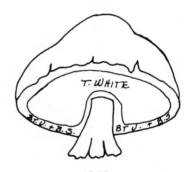

12-10.

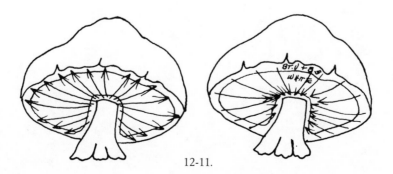

12-11.

Every mushroom has a stem, but not every mushroom has an apron. Both stems and aprons are painted in the same manner:

1. Using a #1 flat brush, undercoat the apron with titanium white as illustrated (Figure 12-12).

2. Wipe the brush and pick up burnt umber plus a little burnt sienna. Apply this color across the top, down the left (dark) side of the apron, and in the two areas at the bottom of the apron as shown (Figure 12-13).

3. Wipe the brush thoroughly, then pat and blend. Follow the natural growth direction of the apron. Study the apron on the color worksheet (Figure C-8).

4. Undercoat the stem in titanium white. Do not paint all the way to the top or all the way down the left (dark) side.

5. Wipe the brush; fill it with burnt umber plus a touch of burnt sienna. Apply this color across the top and down the left (dark) side of the stem.

6. Wipe the brush and gently blend up and down, following the natural direction of the stem.

Here are some helpful tips for painting mushrooms:

1. Contrast is *so* important. Keep the dark areas dark, gently and gradually blending into lighter values, then into white. This is why I don't like to undercoat with a light color all the way out to the edges of a pattern: if a dark color is applied on top of a light color and blended, as a rule the dark color will lose much of its depth. Study the color worksheet and practice!

2. If you have a great deal of difficulty in painting the mushroom gills, you can colorbook-paint the gill area in titanium white plus burnt umber. Let dry. Using burnt umber thinned to a thin consistency and a #1 liner, paint fine, hair-like lines on the undercoated gill area.

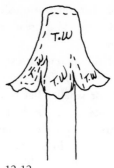

12-12.

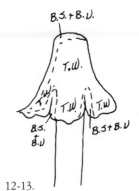

12-13.

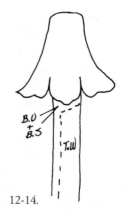

12-14.

GRASS

Grass is simple to paint yet extremely effective if done neatly and carefully.

Use a #4 or larger ph flat red-sable tole brush. Grass colors are titanium white and/or brilliant yellow light, cadmium yellow medium, Shiva leaf green, Prussian blue, and burnt umber.

Here is how to paint grass:

1. Along the grass area dab on leaf green, using a #4 brush.

2. Wipe the brush; pick up a little cadmium yellow medium. Dab under the leaf green.

3. Wipe the brush. Pick up a little titanium white. Dab under the yellow.

4. Wipe the brush. Add a touch of burnt umber plus Prussian blue on top of the leaf green. Wipe the brush thoroughly or use a soft, dry brush. Pat and blend the colors together slightly (Figure C-8).

5. Wipe the brush and pinch the hairs together between your fingers so that the brush holds a *good* flat edge. Pick up a little more leaf green, then slide the flat edge of your brush up through the applied colors, painting streaks of grass. Paint some of the grass in clumps, with several blades stemming from the same spot.

Here are some helpful tips for painting grass:

1. Let some streaks be tall and some short.

2. Let some streaks curve right and some left.

3. Keep pinching the brush together to hold a good flat edge and pick up more leaf green as needed.

4. Do not apply paint too thickly.

5. Keep clumps of grass as thin as possible.

12-15.

12-16.

12-17.

12-18.

12-19. Right.

12-20. Wrong.

NOTE: WHEN PAINTING GRASS PAINT IN "CLUMPS" LET SEVERAL STALKS OF GRASS STEM FROM THE SAME POINT.

12-21.

"COMMON POINTS"

Violets

Violets are a joy to paint—they are delicate and dainty if properly done. When they are crudely painted, however, they do not resemble violets at all. If you follow my directions, the violets that you paint will delight you. They should be painted by all who love to paint and enjoyed by all who love beauty.

The violet is a brushstroke flower that is painted with the flat brush. Like all brushstroke flowers, it is relatively quick to paint *if* you have practiced and learned the basic brushstrokes with the flat brush. The centers take a little longer to paint, as they are small and require a certain amount of concentrated detail.

A violet has five petals, four of which should be made in single strokes. You can go back over the stroke if necessary, but, if the petal can be made with a single stroke, the finished effect will be lovelier. The fifth petal of the violet is called the lead petal. The V-shaped center of the violet always opens onto the lead petal. This petal is always a little larger than the others and requires more than one stroke to paint. In painting violets *do not double-load your brush*. Double-loading makes the violet look like a pinwheel.

Use a #1 ph flat red-sable tole brush and a #1 ph liner. For blue violets use titanium white and Prussian blue. For purple violets use titanium white and dioxyzine purple or violet. For white violets use titanium white, Shiva yellow citron, and raw sienna.

Color-loading techniques are demonstrated on the color worksheet (Figure C-9). Proper loading of the brush is of great importance in painting violets. Loading for the desired color should be practiced many times before you actually paint violets on an item.

For blue violets stroke through a little Prussian blue, then stroke through titanium white. The colors should be streaked together in the brush. Control the shade of blue by adding more or less Prussian blue.

For purple violets load the brush in the same manner with purple or violet and titanium white. I like to mix the violet colors by stroking through a little blue, then purple, then white.

For white violets load the brush in the same manner by stroking through a little Shiva yellow citron and raw sienna, then stroking through titanium white. The white should be dominant, with just a little color showing.

Here is how to paint the four back petals:

1. Fill the brush with the proper colors.

2. Touch the *outside edge* of a petal, apply pressure on the brush, pull, and lift up on the flat edge of the brush to form somewhat of a point at the center of the violet.

3. Continue to paint the other three back petals in the same manner.

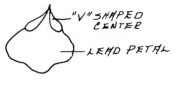

13-1.

13-2.

13-3. Touch.

13-4. Apply pressure.

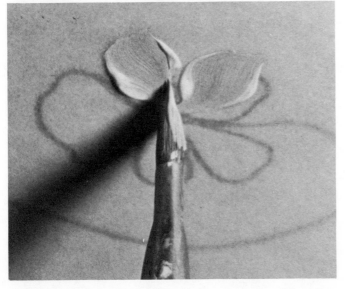

13-5. Lift up on the flat edge of the brush at the center of the violet.

Here is how to paint the lead petal:

1. Double-load the #1 flat brush with the main violet color and titanium white.

2. Scallop or outline around the outside edges of the lead petal. The white should be to the outside; a slight ridge of white around the outside edge is optional but certainly desirable.

3. Wipe the brush and reload by stroking through the colors that you are using. Stroke in the rest of the petal. This will require more than one stroke; blend a little if needed. (This is the only place where blending is recommended on the violet.) Be sure to blend with a light touch—light pressure on the brush.

13-6. It is easier to scallop in the white if you turn the lead petal so that the top of it is away from you.

13-7. Blend lightly from top to bottom and from bottom to top.

The violet center is painted with a #1 ph liner brush and cadmium yellow light, burnt umber, titanium white, and cadmium red pale:

1. Carefully paint the inside of the V in cadmium yellow light.

2. Fill in the two tiny, commalike strokes with titanium white.

3. Outline both the inside and the outside of these tiny white strokes with a fine, hairlike line of burnt umber.

4. Place a tiny dot of cadmium red pale in the throat of the yellow V.

5. Paint fine, hairlike lines of the main color on the *three front petals* of each violet. If you have painted blue violets, use Prussian blue for the linework; for purple violets use the darkest shade of purple.

To do linework, use an excellent liner or a fine-pointed brush and *thin your color with turp to a thin consistency so that the paint will flow easily from the tip of the brush.* The brush *must* be completely full of paint. You can make or break your violet with linework. It must be good, and all the lines should come from a central point on each petal. Practice linework every day.

Here are some helpful tips for painting violets:

1. Paint the violets to the back of the design much darker than violets to the front. Definite contrast between light and dark violets will add depth and dimension to the design.

2. Remember that the violet is a stroke flower, and stroke flowers require little or no blending. Do not muddy violet colors by overblending.

3. Load the brush properly with colors, then test-stroke on the palette before painting the violet petal.

4. Practice the violet center on your palette before painting it on your design.

The violet leaf's heart shape makes it easy to paint. I like to use the basic brushstroke drybrush-blend leaf technique. Simply block in the leaf shape, using the basic brushstroke techniques, add colors, then blend. If a leaf lies under a violet, shade it darker in that area. Contrast is important.

13-8.

13-9.

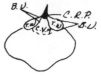

13-10.

13-11.

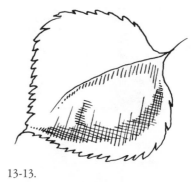

13-12.

LINE WORK MUST COME FROM A CENTRAL POINT - AND GRACEFULLY FLOW OUT ONTO EACH PETAL.

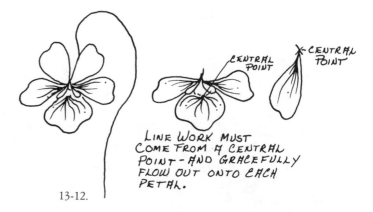

13-13.

The Basic Rose

The rose is one of the loveliest flowers taught in tole and decorative painting. It is a little more difficult than some other flowers only because it requires thorough understanding and much practice of basic brushstrokes and double-loading techniques with the flat brush.

If you compare the basic rose with the advanced rose, you may be tempted to skip the basic-rose lesson in favor of the more beautiful advanced pink rose. Take my advice—don't do it! My basic-rose technique was developed as a foundation for the advanced-rose technique. There is a reason for each step. Your work will be more beautiful, and you will be a happier painter if you follow my suggestions.

In teaching the basic rose in regular classes I ask the students to paint fifty basic roses on tracing paper. This practice prepares them for more advanced rose techniques. I promise you that, if you understand the construction of the basic rose and put forth a little effort to practice, you will paint beautiful roses. The color worksheet (Figure C-9) will take you step-by-step through the painting of the basic rose.

A rose is framed by its leaves. Since one basic rose by itself is not particularly beautiful, paint some leaves along with your practice roses. They will enhance the roses and make painting them more fun.

Use flat brushes. The size of the brush depends on the size of the rose to be painted. For this lesson use a #4 ph flat red-sable tole brush in *excellent* condition. Don't even try to paint a rose with a brush that is in poor condition. For this job the brush must be as perfect as possible.

For the pink rose use titanium white, Shiva red crimson, and burnt umber. Add just a touch of burnt umber to the Shiva red crimson for a deep, rich color. For the yellow rose use titanium white, cadmium yellow light and/or cadmium yellow medium, and raw sienna. Add a touch of raw sienna to the yellow to give it more depth.

The consistency of the white *must* be correct for painting roses. Using a palette knife, mix or whip the white with a few drops of turp until the consistency of whipped cream is reached. Remember to check the paint consistency from time to time. *Keep the brush properly loaded.* Always test a double-loaded brush on the palette before actually applying strokes to the rose. Here is how to paint the basic rose:

1. Apply a dot of color in the center of the rose, as shown in Figures 14-1 and 14-2.

14-1.

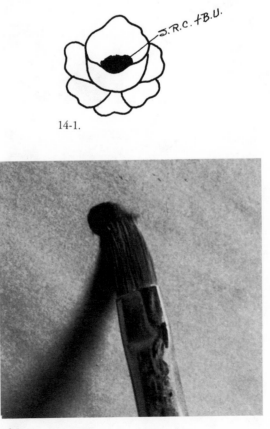

14-2.

2. Double-load the brush with the whipped white and color. Blend on the palette to soften the color. With the white to the outside, stand the brush on the flat edge at the left side of the dot, slide up, apply pressure, and paint an upside-down U around the dot of color, catching the color with the corner of the brush and pulling or blending the color up into the petals. (If you are right-handed, stroke from left to right; if left-handed, from right to left.) You may go back over this stroke as many times as needed. While holding pressure on the brush, follow the pattern of the petal, making the top of the rose appear a little scalloped.

3. To paint the base, or bowl, of the rose, double-load the brush with whipped white and color; blend on the palette to soften the color. Stand the brush on the flat edge at the left side of the rose. The color will be on the bottom. Pull down, apply pressure, and lift back up on the flat edge at the right side of the rose. You may go back over the bowl stroke as many times as you wish.

4. Wipe the brush on a rag and pick up more white on the white side of the brush. Carefully paint a scalloplike stroke under the center of the rose. Be careful not to touch any of the color. *If necessary*, you may wipe your brush and blend the base or bowl a little.

5. The next step is to paint five petals around the base of the rose. You will find this easier to do if you turn the rose upside down and paint the petals around the base from left to right. Double-load the brush with whipped white and color. *The white is to the outside.* Paint five quarter-circle strokes around the base of the rose. The third stroke is the middle stroke and should be located in the center of the base. *Do not make these petal strokes too large.* This is a common mistake that should be avoided.

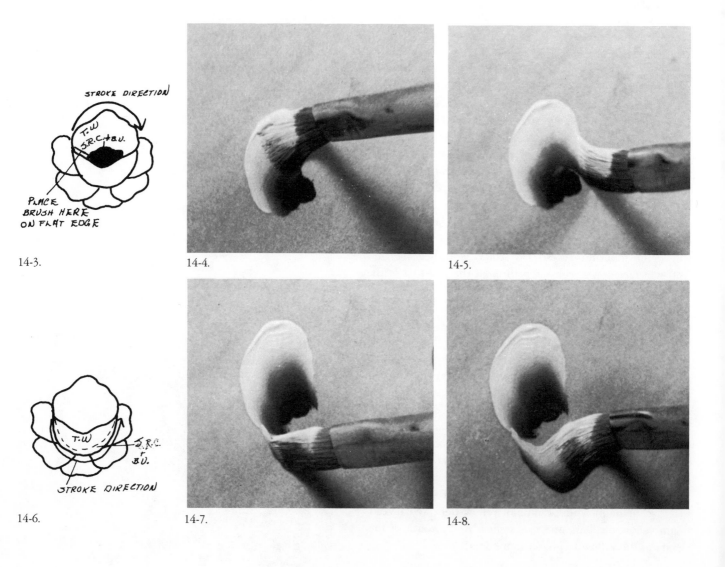

14-3.

14-4.

14-5.

14-6.

14-7.

14-8.

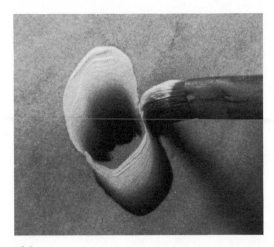

14-9.

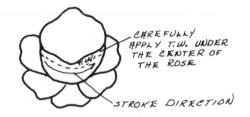
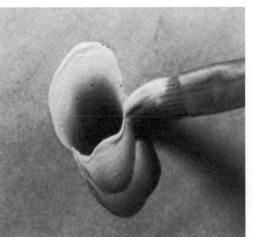

CAREFULLY APPLY T.W. UNDER THE CENTER OF THE ROSE

STROKE DIRECTION

14-10.

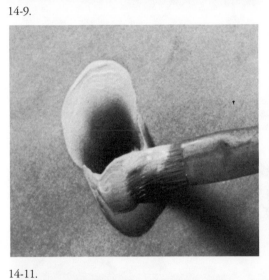

14-11.

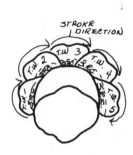

STROKE DIRECTION

T.W. 2   T.W. 3
T.W.   STRK   T.W. 4
STRK   T.W. 1   STRK   T.W. 5

14-12.

14-13.

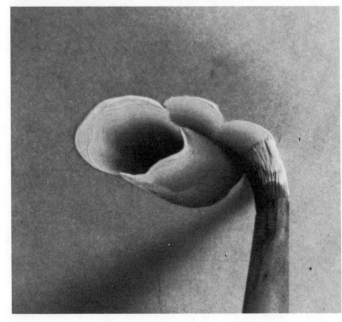

14-14.

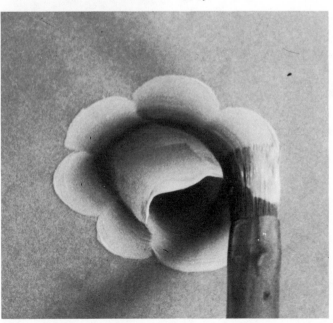

14-15.

Rosebuds are much easier to paint than a complete rose. I think of them as very dainty in appearance. A few little buds with some trailing blue ribbon is always a special added touch, and it can be achieved in a hurry if you know the technique. Brushes and colors are the same as for the basic rose.

The open rosebud is the basic rose completed through step 4. The base of the bud, the stem, and the bracts around the bud must be added. The base and bracts are painted in leaf green and shaded with a little burnt umber to the left and a little white to the right (see Figure C-9). The stem is painted with the liner brush. It is green, with an outline of burnt umber to the left and an outline of white to the

right. Wipe the liner brush and lightly blend the three colors together.

The closed rosebud is nothing more than a tiny basic leaf, shaded with the rose color to the left and with white to the right (see Figure C-9). The bud base, bracts, and stem should be added as described above—and don't forget to add a *tiny* burnt-umber thorn where and when needed.

A #4 brush is used for leaves, as shown on the color worksheet (Figure C-9). The rose leaf is generally painted with the basic brushstroke drybrush-blend technique. Remember to use a lot of contrast in your leaves. Let them live. Do not overblend them.

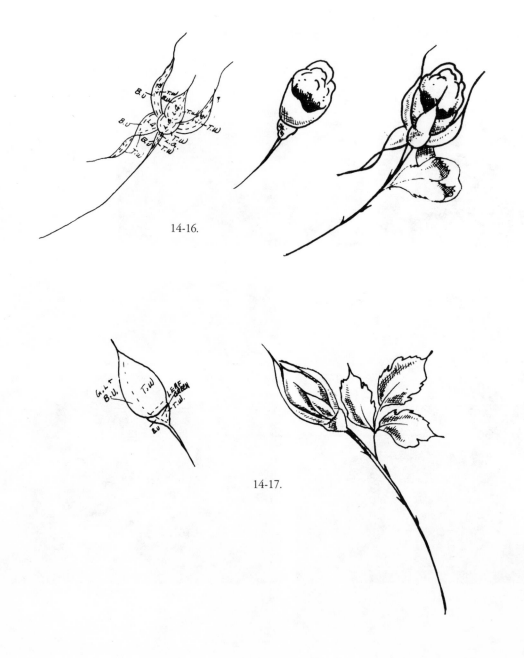

14-16.

14-17.

70

The Advanced Rose

In the beginning tole and decorative painting wasn't easy for me. I wanted to paint roses more than anything in the world, and how proud I was of the old tin salt shaker! I painted it white, antiqued it brown, and painted brown roses and brown leaves on it. That old salt shaker graced our table for many years. Is it ever bad! The roses *do* look like horse manure and the leaves look like lettuce leaves, but I loved it because I had done it. It is a far cry from the roses that I paint today. I have never had a student who painted roses as badly as I did the first time I tried them, but I wasn't taught "how to" in the way I teach you!

15-2 and 15-3. The advanced rose.

15-1. My first rose.

In order to paint the advanced rose, you must understand the complete construction of the rose—the way a rose is put together. You must know and understand basic brushstrokes with the flat brush and double-loading techniques. You must have a brush in *excellent* condition. Proper loading of the brush with the correct colors is of the utmost importance. It takes study and practice to learn all this properly, but it is all here for you, in both black-and-white photographs and full color. If you put forth a little effort, I can guarantee results.

Remember—the following steps are vital to the successful painting of a beautiful rose:

1. Your brush must be of the finest quality and in excellent condition.

2. Know and practice all the basic brushstrokes with the flat brush.

3. Understand and practice double-loading the flat brush.

4. Thoroughly review the basic-rose technique. If you have not painted at least fifty basic roses, you should do so before attempting to paint the advanced rose. The experience that you will gain in controlling paint consistency and contrast will be of great value to you, as will practice of the strokes used in the basic rose.

5. Follow my instructions *slowly* and *completely*, step by step, photograph by photograph, and study the exam-ples on the worksheet (Figures C-10 and C-11).

Use a #10 ph flat red-sable tole brush in *excellent* condition. Colors are Shiva red crimson, burnt umber, titanium white, and brilliant yellow light. Mix a touch of burnt umber with Shiva red crimson (see the example on the color worksheet). Mix together equal parts of titanium white and brilliant yellow light. Cream the paint with turp or copal medium to the consistency of whipped cream. It should actually hold peaks.

Here is how to paint the advanced rose:

1. Double-load the brush with the white mixture on one side and the pink mixture on the other. Blend on the palette to soften the color. Be sure that the brush is full of paint and that the paint is of the proper consistency to flow freely from the brush.

2. Paint the center stroke of the back row of petals. *The white is always to the outside in painting the petals.* This is a scalloped stroke, not a U-shaped stroke.

3. Paint a commalike stroke to the right of the center stroke. This stroke must lift to a beautiful flat edge as you come toward the center of the rose.

4. Paint the same type of stroke on the left-hand side of the rose.

5. Check the strokes that you have painted to be sure that the pink color is good and strong. If not, now is the time to go back over each stroke carefully to strengthen the color.

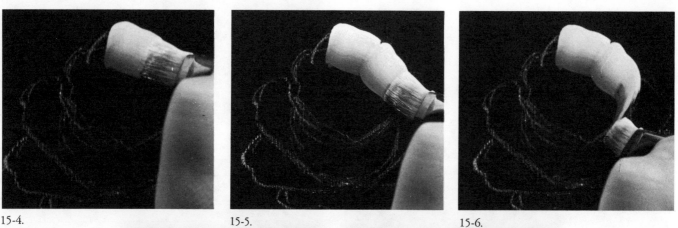

15-4.   15-5.   15-6.

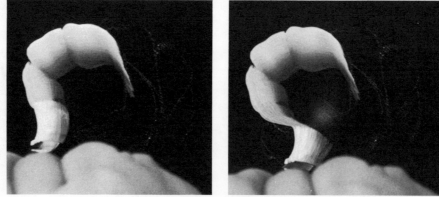

15-7.   15-8.

6. Lay a second row of petals on top of the back row. When this second row is painted, the white edge must show against the pink of the first row of petals. Refer to the color worksheet (Figures C-10 and C-11). The brush is still double-loaded with the white mixture and the pink mixture, as it is throughout the painting of the rose. Keep the strokes high. Follow the placement of these strokes in the photographs, then study this step on the color worksheet.

7. Paint the first base, or bowl, of the rose with the edges connecting to the edges of the second row of petals as illustrated. Start on the left side, stroking from left to right. Stand the brush on the flat edge where it touches the second row of petals. Slide down and apply pressure. Hold the pressure and scallop across the top, lifting up on the flat edge of the brush and connecting to the second row of petals on the right-hand side. (If you are left-handed, reverse the instructions.)

8. Paint the outside petals. Place the double-loaded brush so that the stroke appears to come from behind the upper row of petals. Place the brush just slightly above the center of the rose. This is a big commatype stroke, and you must lift up on the flat edge of the brush as you come into the base of the rose. You may paint three, five, or six outside petals. I usually paint five. Study the photographs of each stroke. Go back over the strokes to strengthen the color, if needed. Continue to check the paint consistency to be sure that it is correct. Proper paint consistency is vital to your success.

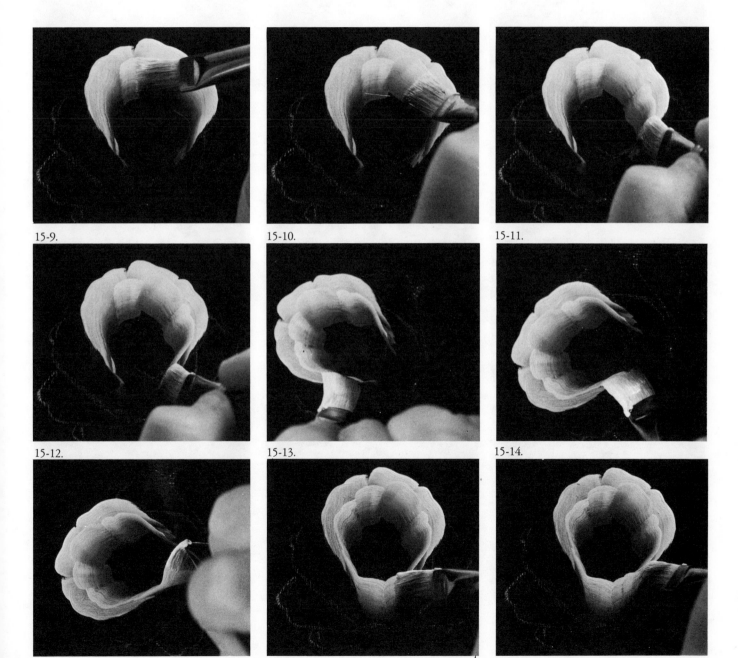

15-9.

15-10.

15-11.

15-12.

15-13.

15-14.

15-15.

15-16.

15-17.

9. Paint the second base, or bowl, across the front of the rose. Stand the brush on the flat edge on the left-hand side where it joins the edge of the back row of petals. Again, pull down and scallop over the first base of the rose. Lift up on the flat edge of the brush on the right-hand side where the bowl joins the first row of petals. If necessary, you may go back over this stroke, but do not go back over it any more than is absolutely necessary.

15-18.

15-19.

15-20.

15-21.

15-22.

15-23.

15-24.

15-25.

15-26.

15-27.

15-28.

15-29.

15-30.

15-31.

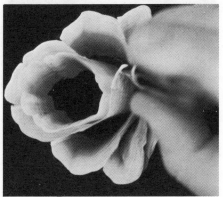

15-32.

15-33.

15-34.

15-35.

15-36.

10. Fill-in petals are painted on top of the outside row of petals. Be sure that you have good strong color on the outside row so that the fill-in petals will show up. They are made with commalike strokes; it is important to lift up on the flat edge of the brush as you tuck them in the rose. Study the photographs of my strokes and practice painting your strokes over mine. There is no certain number of fill-in petals. I use as many as seem to be needed to complete a beautiful rose, and I never paint two rows in exactly the same way. Pay careful attention to the photographs of each stroke.

11. Paint the rolled petal. Rolling a petal across the base of the rose is not difficult if you are willing to practice. The idea is to connect one edge of the fill-in petal to the edge of another. In doing so a petal is formed that cups up over the base. An S-stroke is used. Study the photograph: you will see where this stroke should be placed. Stand the double-loaded brush on the flat edge, pull, apply pressure, then lift back up on the flat edge. Start from one edge of the petal and connect with another. Study the color worksheet.

12. Now it is time to slice the edges of the petals. This technique can only be learned by practice. The sliced-in

15-37.

15-38.

15-39.

15-40.

15-41.

15-42.

15-43.

15-44.

15-45.

15-46.

15-47.

edges should look like the edges of a rosepetal that is just starting to roll back and open. Think of the slices as connecting the edge of one petal to the edge of another. This is exactly what you are doing. You may occasionally paint a rose with no slices at all, but, as a rule, when you study your completed rose, you will find places where slicing will add greater depth to the petals.

13. The final step is to complete the center of the rose.

a. Double-load the brush with the pink mixture on one side and the white mixture on the other. Blend on the palette to soften the color.

b. With the white to the outside, begin scalloping the third row of petals into the upper portion of the rose center.

c. Wipe the brush. Pick up a little more white and paint small scalloplike strokes at random. Some should be high; some may drop a little lower. Keep the throat of the center very dark. Again, study the photographs and the color worksheet.

15-48.

15-49.

15-50.

15-51.

15-52.

15-53.

15-54.

15-55.

15-56.

The following deliberately exaggerated mistakes are common in painting a rose. To avoid these mistakes:

1. Do not paint severely scalloped strokes.

2. Do not line petals up in a row.

3. Do not put thick tails on commalike strokes that form the outside petals.

4. Do not make the left side of the rose the same shape as the right side.

My favorite leaf for the rose is the basic brushstroke drybrush-blend leaf. In adding colors to the center of the leaf for blending, be sure to add some of the rose color. Remember how vital contrast is to your leaves and keep those to the back of the design much darker than those to the front. Also remember to shade leaves that lie underneath the rose.

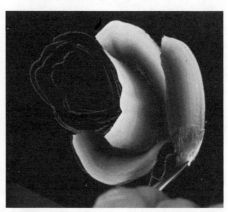

I'll never forget the satisfaction that I felt the first time that I painted a rose well enough to be pleased with it. It took me a long time, but it was truly worth the effort. You can do this, too, just as hundreds of my students have, by following my instructions carefully.

This is only the beginning of tole and decorative painting. In fact, decorative painting and related art forms, such as dimensional glass painting, pen-and-ink, fabric painting, country carving, and miniature-canvas painting, go on and on and on. If I live to be a hundred years old, I'll only be able to do a tiny bit of what I'd like to do in the fascinating world of tole and decorative painting.

One of the greatest joys that a teacher can know is to hear from her students. If you have any questions, if you have problems, or if you have enjoyed what you have learned from this book, let me know. Write to me at P.O. Box 7026, Tulsa, Oklahoma 74105.

The Priscilla Hauser Accredited Teachers and National Representatives are always ready to help you, too. Feel free to call on them.

And now, be happy. Life is full of ups and downs, but remember—with paintbrush in hand, life is emptied of its sorrows, and its beauty smiles.

15-61. I wanted you to see how much blending is done on the palette in painting an advanced rose. Much more time is spent in preparing the brush to paint the strokes of the rose than in the actual painting of the rose itself!

Patterns and Color Worksheets

Following the color worksheets is a collection of ideas and projects for tole and decorative painting. I hope you enjoy each and every one of them!

C-1. Priscilla Hauser's brushstroke directory.

C-2. Priscilla Hauser's basic-leaf and basic-brushstroke-drybrush-blend-leaf worksheet.

C-3. Priscilla Hauser's turned-leaf worksheet.

C-4. Priscilla Hauser's daisy worksheet.

C-5. Priscilla Hauser's lemon and strawberry worksheet.

C-6. Priscilla Hauser's red- and green-apple worksheet.

C-7. Priscilla Hauser's peach and pear worksheet.

C-8. Priscilla Hauser's mushroom and grass worksheet.

C-9. Priscilla Hauser's violet and basic-rose worksheet.

C-10 and C-11. Priscilla Hauser's advanced pink-rose worksheet.

Priscilla Hauser's Brush Stroke Directory

Round Brush Strokes

Liner Brush use thin paint & practice.

These commas were all made with a #3 round brush

Polliwog

Comma to Left

Sometimes commas are called: "Eyebrows" A comma to right

S-stroke with a round brush

Teardrop or elongated commas

Short fat commas

Short fat polliwog

Practice printing

Don't Do These Things ----

Don't be a: Pressure Holder

Don't be a: Picker up too Faster

Don't — Lean to the outside edge.

Flat Brush Strokes

"Basic" Stroke

Line Stroke

Commas

Right Side up U - Upside Down U

Right side up half circle

Upside down half circle

A Form of the U Strokes

The Important "S" Strokes

Basic Penn. Dutch Forms — Combine Strokes & Blending

S.R.C. — C.R.P. — C.O.

Stroke in

C.R.P.

Add colors

Blend

Ball Flower Form

B.S. — C.O.

C.Y.M.

Stroke in

B.S.

C.Y.M

Add color & strokes

Blend

Tulip Form

B.Y.L.

Apply color

P.B. + B.V.   B.Y.L.

Paint "J" strokes

P.B. + B.V.   Blend & Add strokes

Borders with both flat and round brush are so much fun to paint — and they are beautiful.

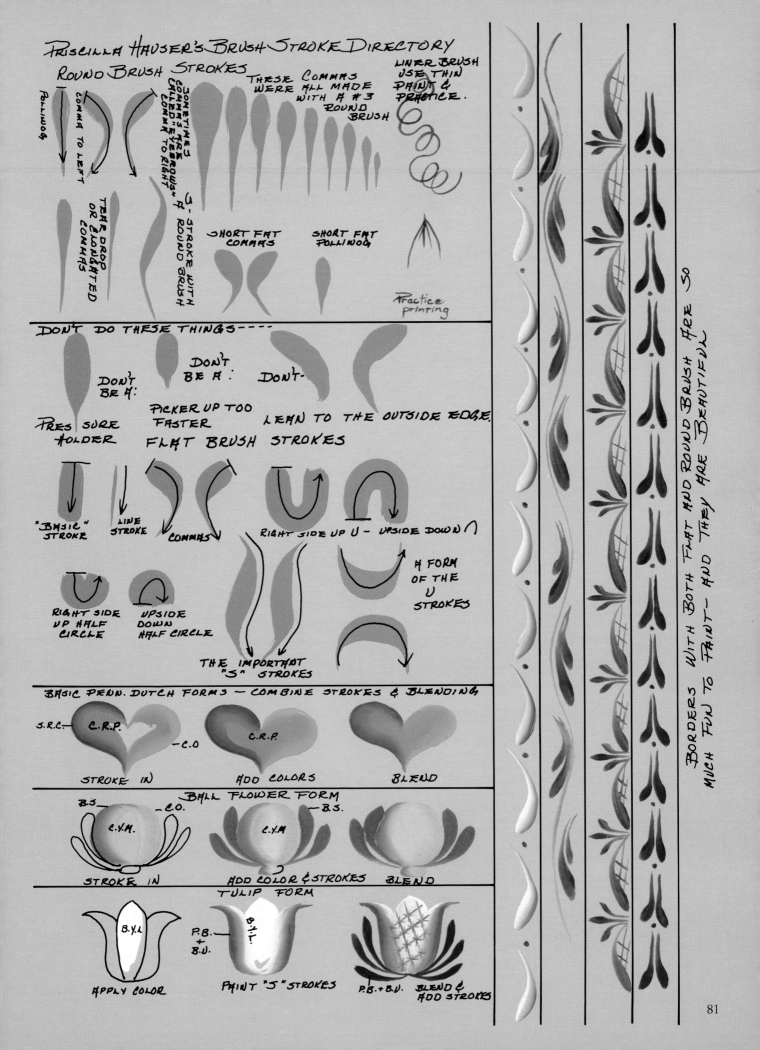

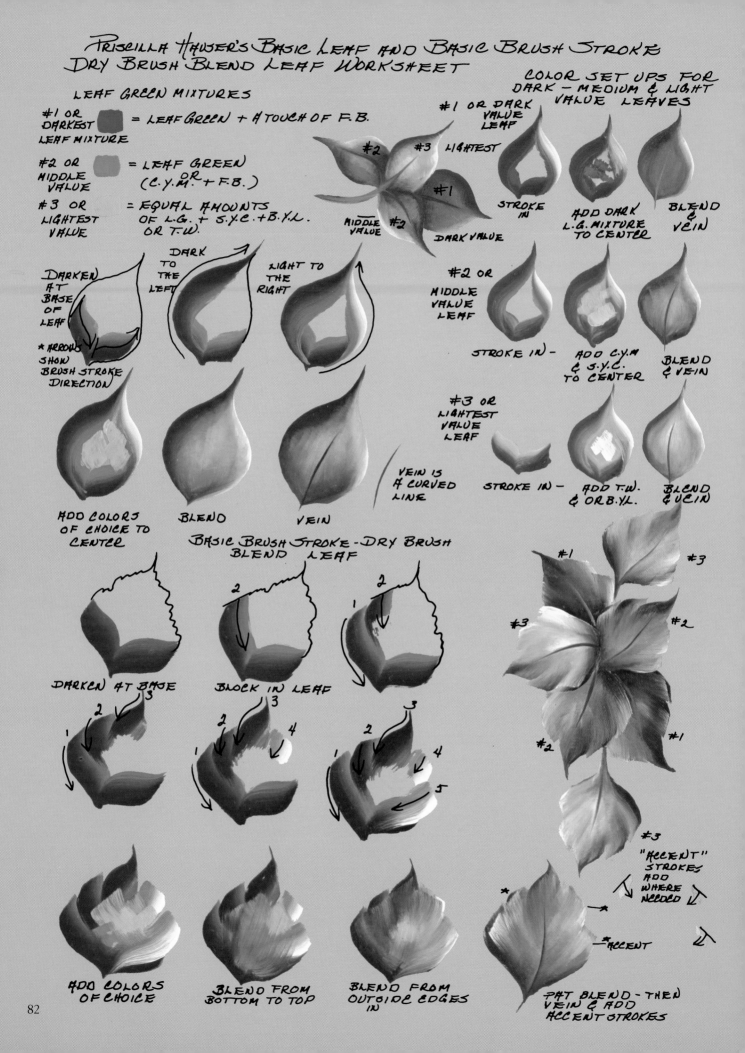

Priscilla Hauser's Basic Leaf and Basic Brush Stroke
Dry Brush Blend Leaf Worksheet

LEAF GREEN MIXTURES

#1 OR DARKEST LEAF MIXTURE = LEAF GREEN + A TOUCH OF F.B.

#2 OR MIDDLE VALUE = LEAF GREEN (C.Y.M. OR + F.B.)

#3 OR LIGHTEST VALUE = EQUAL AMOUNTS OF L.G. + S.Y.C. + B.Y.L. OR T.W.

COLOR SET UPS FOR DARK — MEDIUM & LIGHT VALUE LEAVES

#2 #3 LIGHTEST
#1
MIDDLE VALUE
DARK VALUE

#1 OR DARK VALUE LEAF
STROKE IN — ADD DARK L.G. MIXTURE TO CENTER — BLEND & VEIN

DARKEN AT BASE OF LEAF
*ARROWS SHOW BRUSH STROKE DIRECTION
DARK TO THE LEFT
LIGHT TO THE RIGHT

#2 OR MIDDLE VALUE LEAF
STROKE IN — ADD C.Y.M & S.Y.C. TO CENTER — BLEND & VEIN

ADD COLORS OF CHOICE TO CENTER
BLEND
VEIN

VEIN IS A CURVED LINE

#3 OR LIGHTEST VALUE LEAF
STROKE IN — ADD T.W. & OR B.Y.L. — BLEND & VEIN

Basic Brush Stroke - Dry Brush Blend Leaf

DARKEN AT BASE
BLOCK IN LEAF
2
1
2
3
1
2
3
4
1
2
3
4
5

#1
#3
#3
#2
#2
#1

#3
"ACCENT" STROKES ADD WHERE NEEDED

*
*
—ACCENT

ADD COLORS OF CHOICE
BLEND FROM BOTTOM TO TOP
BLEND FROM OUTSIDE EDGES IN
PAT BLEND - THEN VEIN & ADD ACCENT STROKES

82

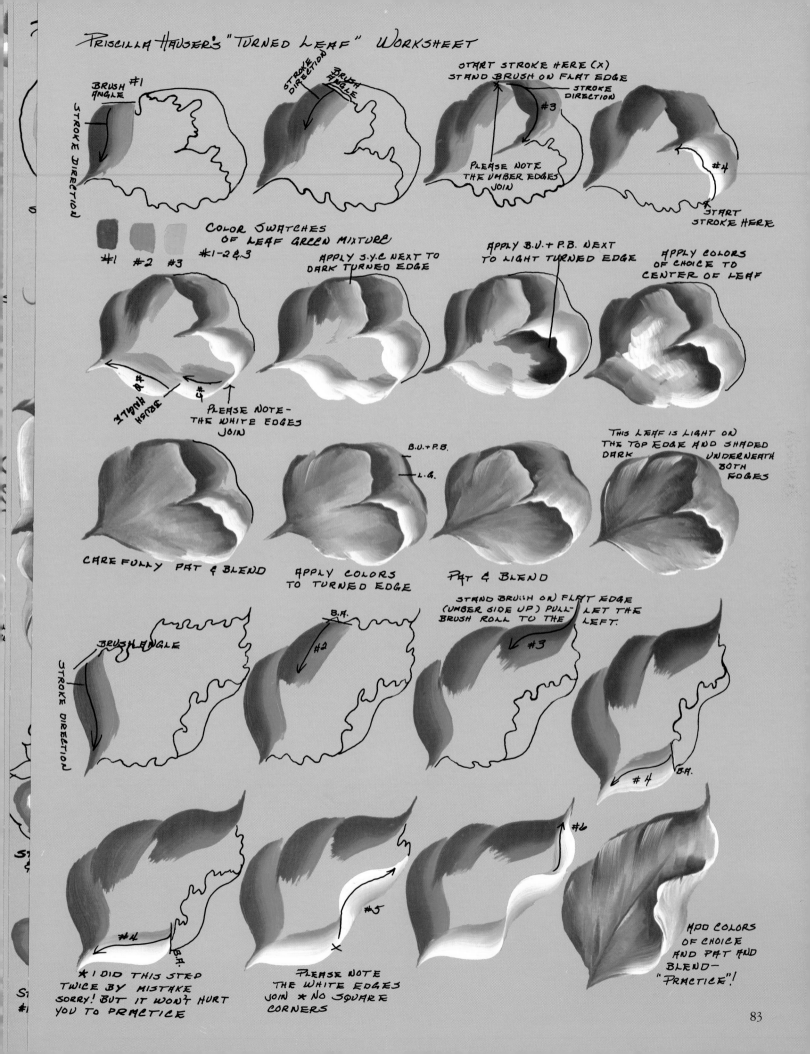

Priscilla Hauser's "Turned Leaf" Worksheet

BRUSH #1
BRUSH ANGLE
STROKE DIRECTION

STROKE DIRECTION
BRUSH ANGLE

START STROKE HERE (X)
STAND BRUSH ON FLAT EDGE
STROKE DIRECTION
#3
PLEASE NOTE THE UMBER EDGES JOIN

#4
START STROKE HERE

Color Swatches of Leaf Green Mixture
#1-2&3
#1 #2 #3

APPLY S.Y.C. NEXT TO DARK TURNED EDGE

APPLY B.U + P.B. NEXT TO LIGHT TURNED EDGE

APPLY COLORS OF CHOICE TO CENTER OF LEAF

BRUSH ANGLE
PLEASE NOTE- THE WHITE EDGES JOIN

CAREFULLY PAT & BLEND

B.U.+P.B.
L.G.
APPLY COLORS TO TURNED EDGE

PAT & BLEND

THIS LEAF IS LIGHT ON THE TOP EDGE AND SHADED DARK UNDERNEATH BOTH EDGES

BRUSH ANGLE
STROKE DIRECTION

B.A.
#2

STAND BRUSH ON FLAT EDGE (UMBER SIDE UP) PULL- LET THE BRUSH ROLL TO THE LEFT.
#3

#4
B.A.

#6

#4
B.A.

#5
X

ADD COLORS OF CHOICE AND PAT AND BLEND- "PRACTICE"!

*I DID THIS STEP TWICE BY MISTAKE SORRY! BUT IT WON'T HURT YOU TO PRACTICE

PLEASE NOTE THE WHITE EDGES JOIN * NO SQUARE CORNERS

C-12.

C-13.

C-14.

C-12. Tin trays and wooden plaques with usable items attached. Under the strawberry hangs a little bract picker. The painted back of a muffin tin makes a darling wall hanging.

C-13. Strawberries and black-eyed-susans painted on small wooden projects are excellent for beginners. The pink rose is a little more advanced. It is painted on an oval piece of Masonite, then mounted inside an old box lid. I call it a box-lid frame.

C-14. Lap desks make beautiful gifts for friends and family. If you are planning on selling your work, you will find that a lap desk is an item that people like to buy. I glued a quote on the daisy-and-lemon lap desk, then painted around it.

C-15. The white roses are painted on a replica of an antique candle box. A little bird house is as cheery and cute as can be. Wooden hangers make charming gifts and will certainly grace a guest closet. They are even attractive in wall groupings. The board with painted apples and daisies has wooden pegs for hanging coats and sweaters.

C-16. A letter box, an old cheese box, and a darling wooden basket. The basket may be used for plants, candy, decorated eggs or even as an Easter basket—and, of course, it will last a lifetime.

C-17. Ladderback chairs are a pleasure to look at. Paint a dining-table chair for each member of your family. They will love it.

C-18. These little keepsake cabinets have shelves to house all kinds of treasures. The scene in the center of each design is done in pen-and-ink. Gold leaf was used behind the lemons. Projects like this are such fun to paint!

C-19. The tole sampler is done on a patchwork board and combines pen-and-ink and decorative painting. I stained and sealed the board, then painted each of the four sections with one of my acrylic-base-coat colors. This design can also be fabric-painted and would make a darling pillow. Use patches of real calico. The tavern sign will welcome all your guests. It is lovely in a hall grouping. A dry-measure spoon hangs from a nail on this daisy board.

C-15.

C-16.

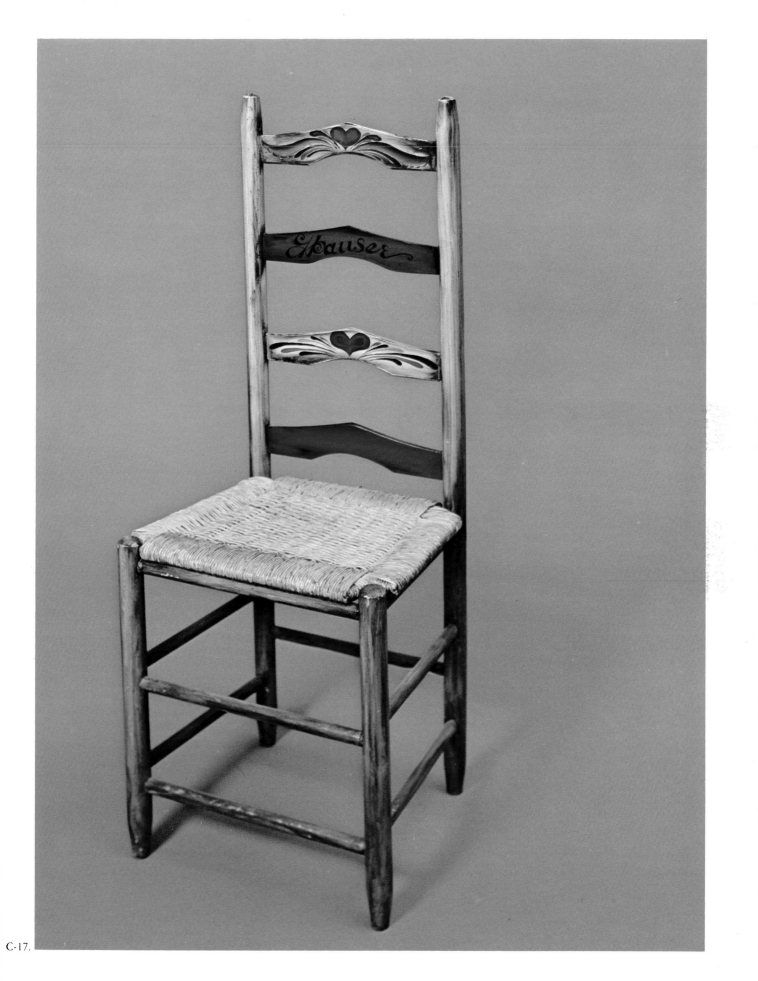

C-18.

C-19.

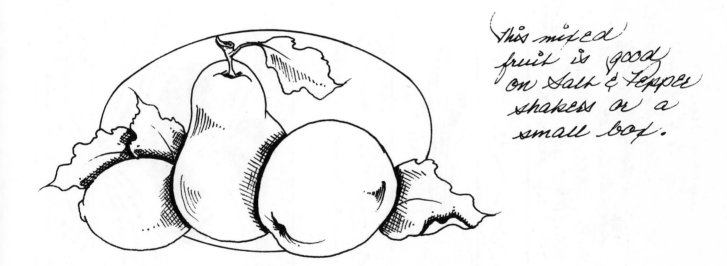

This mixed fruit is good on Salt & Pepper shakers or a small box.

16-1.

Napkin rings in tin are great. These designs much the salt & pepper shakers as they are great border designs ya furniture simply repeat design.

This was designed for a tin salt & pepper shaker. You can print the family name in the center of the heart or the words SALT & PEPPER also

This is lovely on the lid of ya little teapot border design all the way around the lid.

A.M.H.

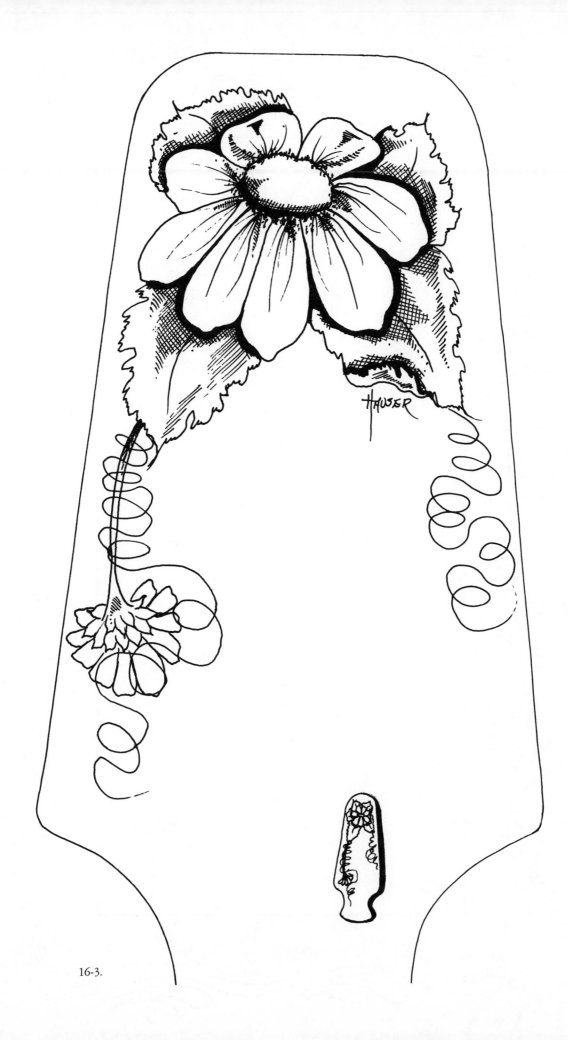

16-3.

Border for top of basket or box

16-4.

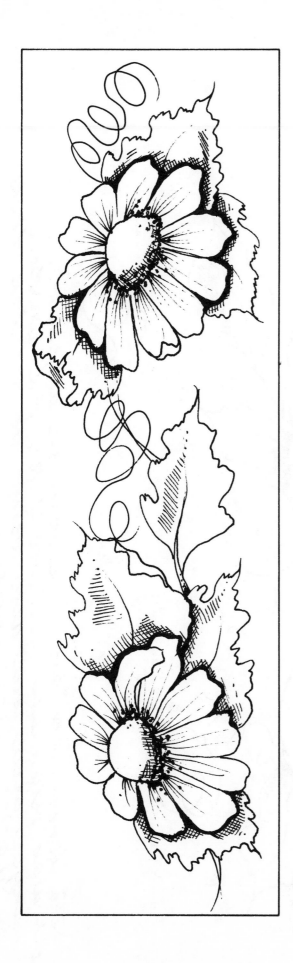

Wooden baskets--
Useful in many ways--
a planter;
child's Easter basket:
even mail or
Christmas cards.

16-5.

This was drawn for the top of a recipe box.

This lemon design is lovely on a purse. It was originally designed for the wooden hanger and will also serve as a lap desk or wooden stool pattern.

16-7.

Work with very simple designs in the beginning - this is very important.

16-8.

16-9.

This design is so cute on a Bird House or Mail Box

16-10.

This is a gorgeous pattern when painted.

16-11.

107

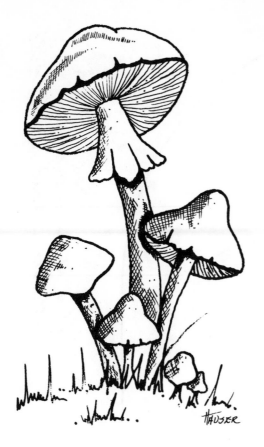

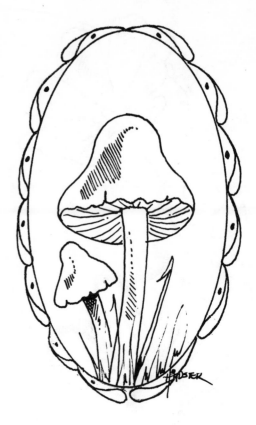

16-12.

A good
"learning"
design

16-13.

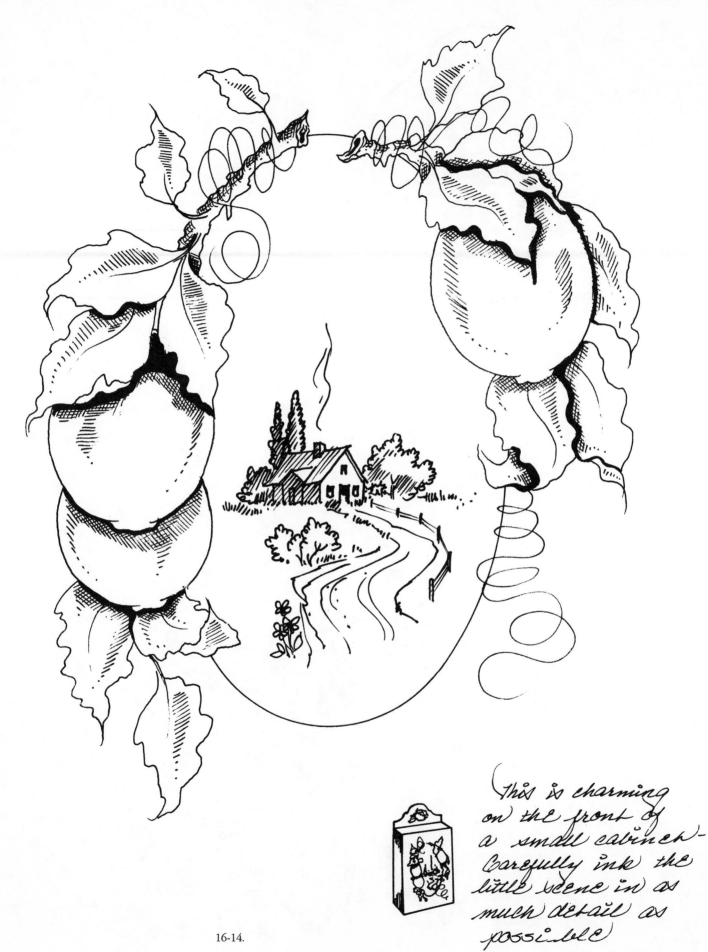

16-14.

This is charming
on the front of
a small cabinet.
Carefully ink the
little scene in as
much detail as
possible.

16-15.

16-16.

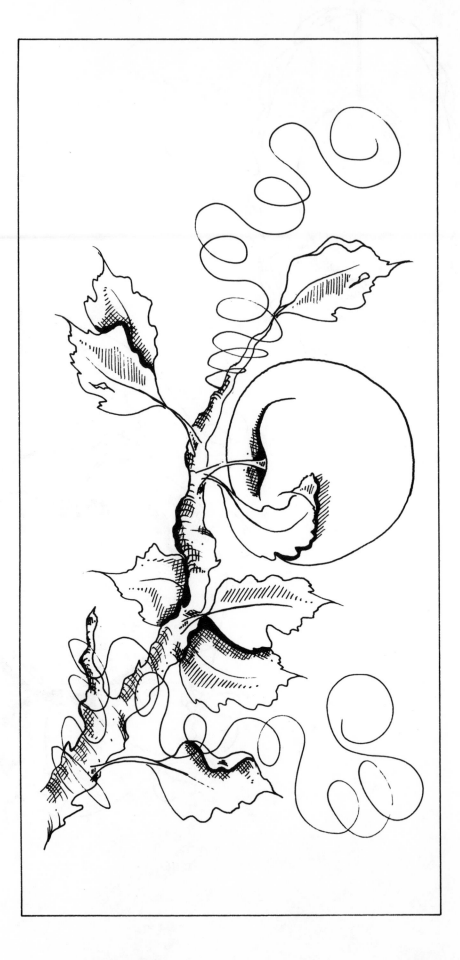

16-17.

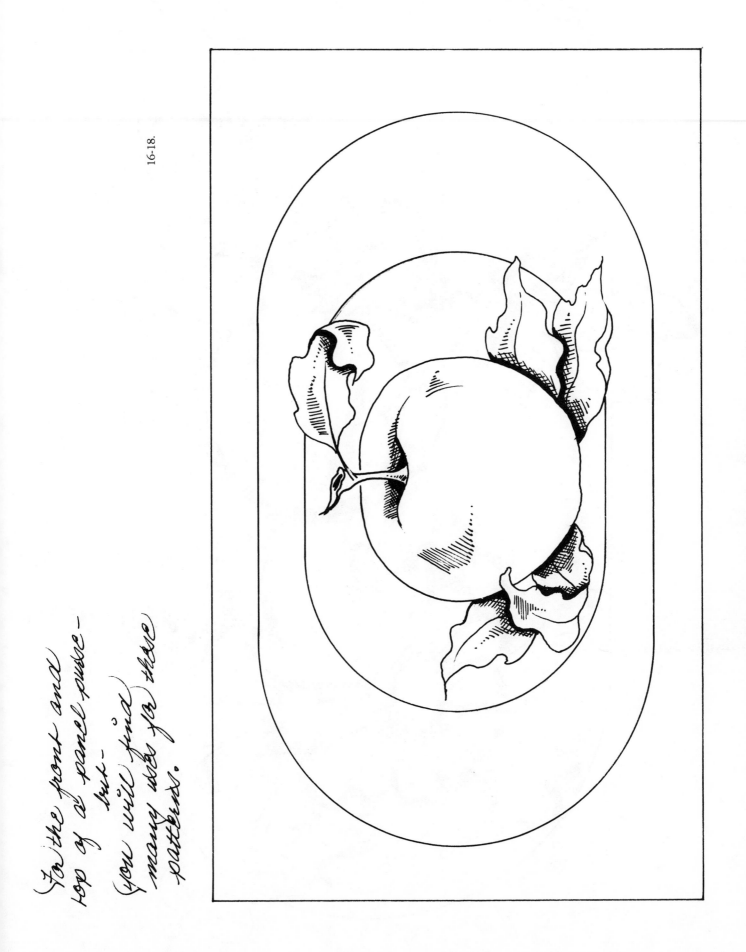

For the front and
top of a panel purse —
but —
(you will find
many uses for these
patterns.

16-18.

113

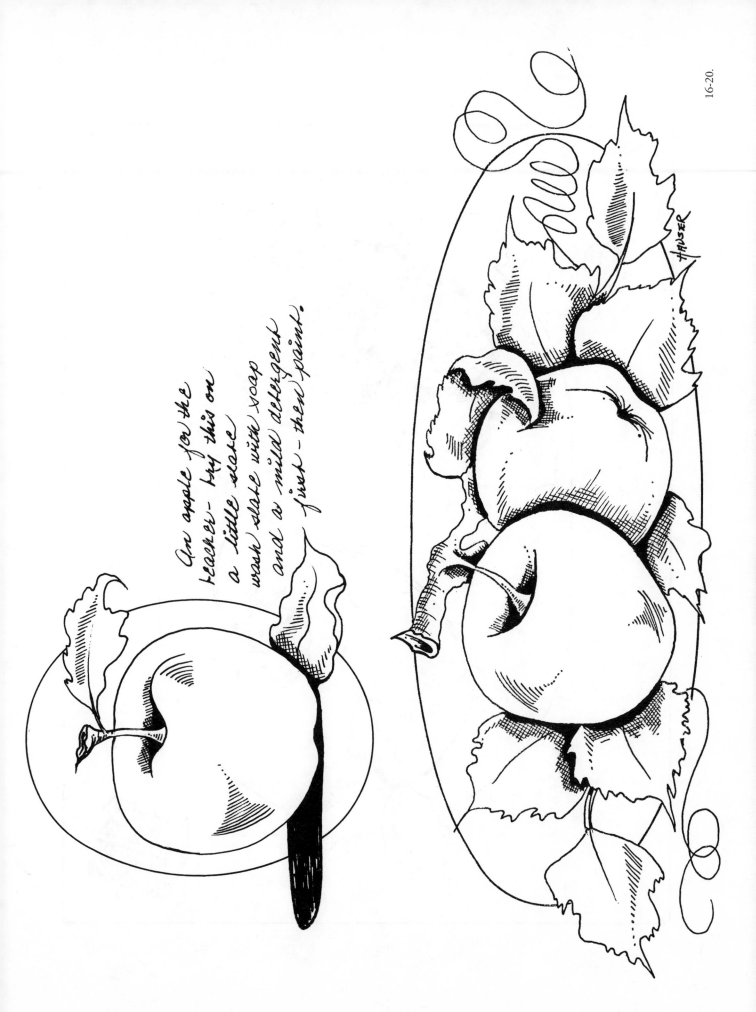

An apple for the
teacher — try this on
a little slate
wash slate with soap
and a mild detergent
first — then paint.

HAUSER

16-21.

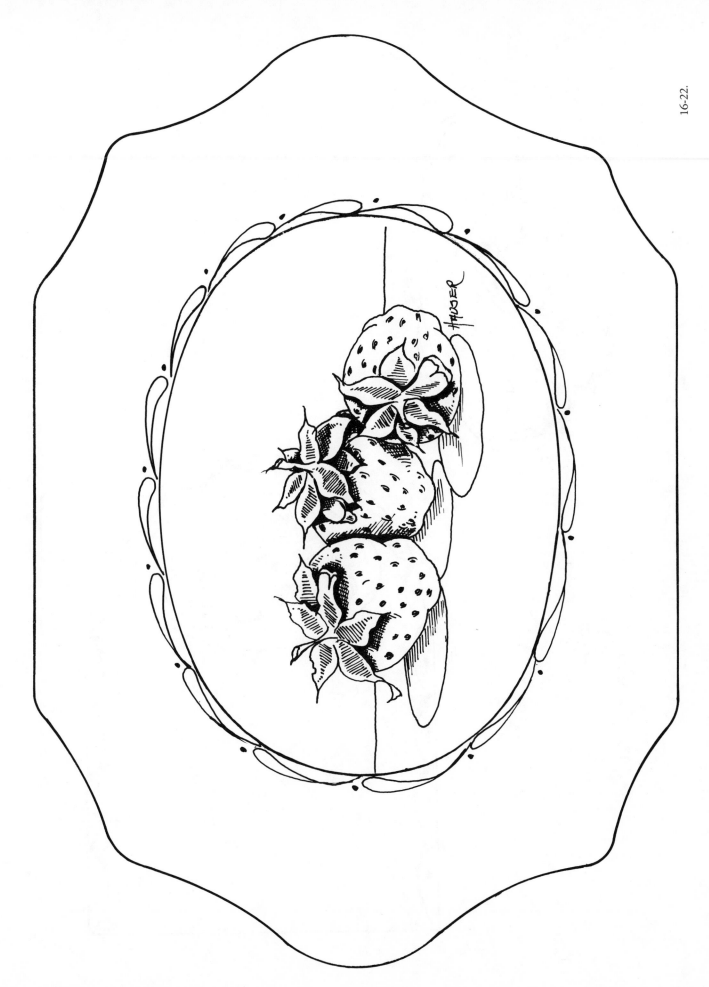

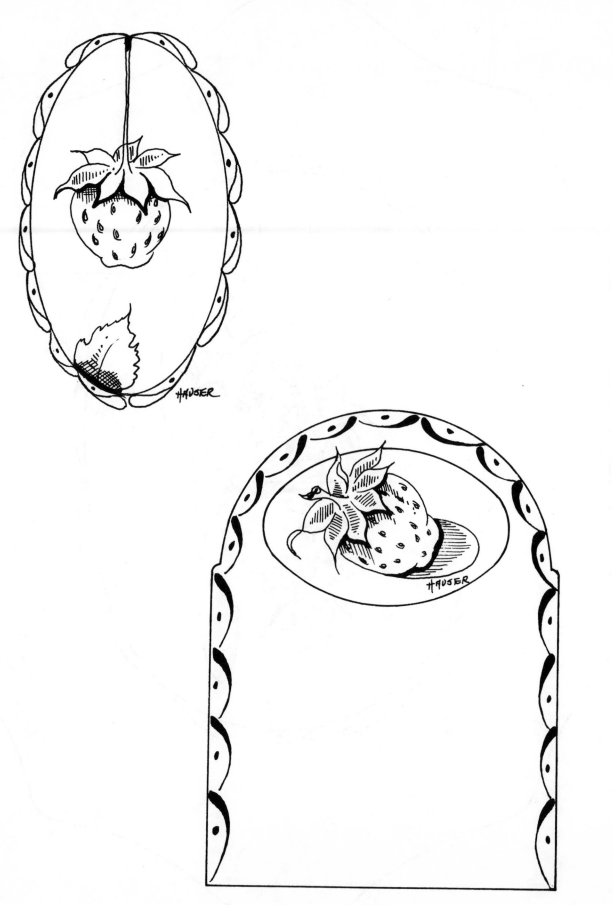

16-23.

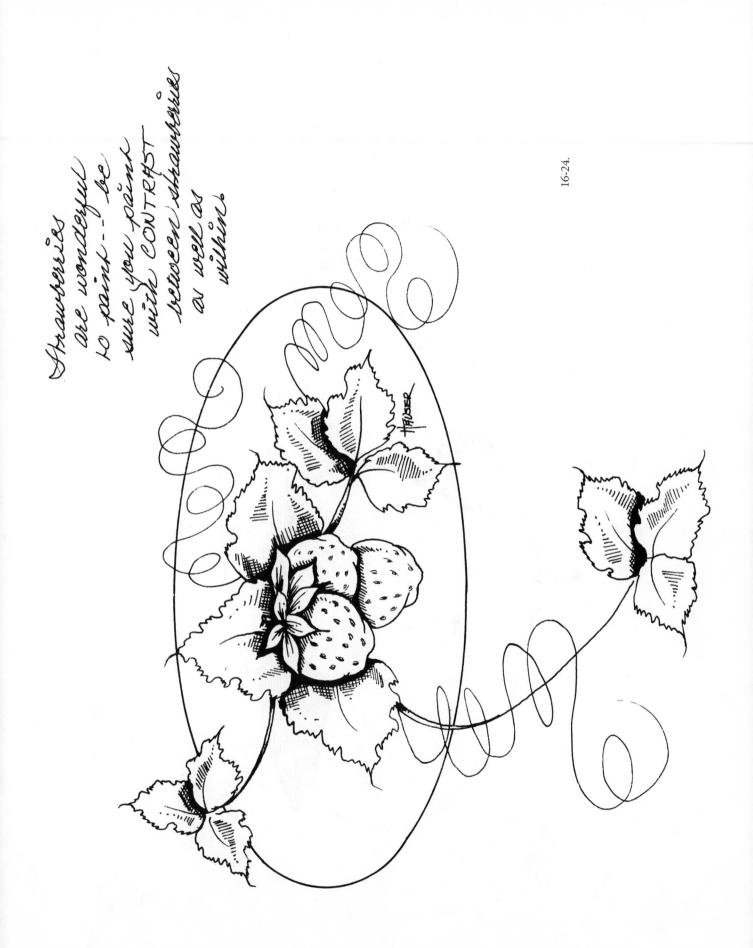

Strawberries are wonderful to paint -- be sure you paint with CONTRAST between strawberries as well as within.

16-24.

119

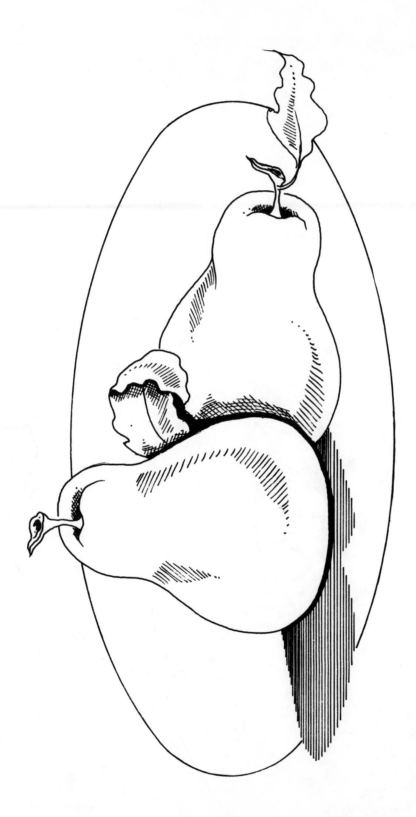

16-25.

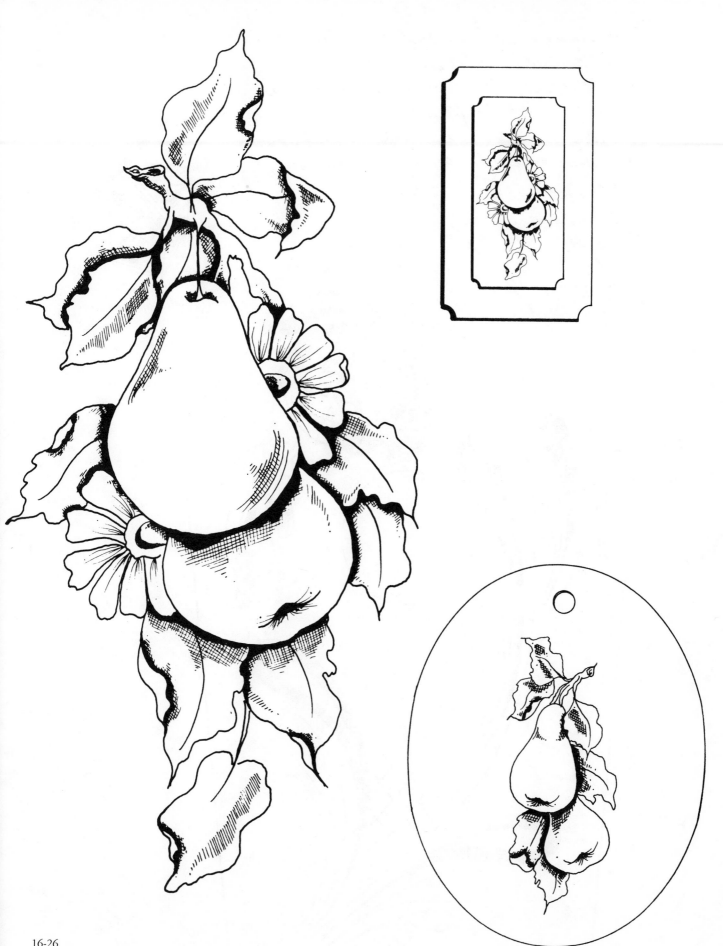

16-26.

You must paint a bird house ---
but these designs are
wonderful for many - many
items - Don't forget -
Penn Dutch needs borders
of "strokes" used with
the main
pattern.
Borders
add a
lot!

16-27.

Paint this on a salt
& pepper shaker - or
small box --- your
name may be used
in the center of the
heart--
    also-
      enlarged
        its lovely
          on the
          front
          door as
        a name
        plate.

HAUSER

16-28.

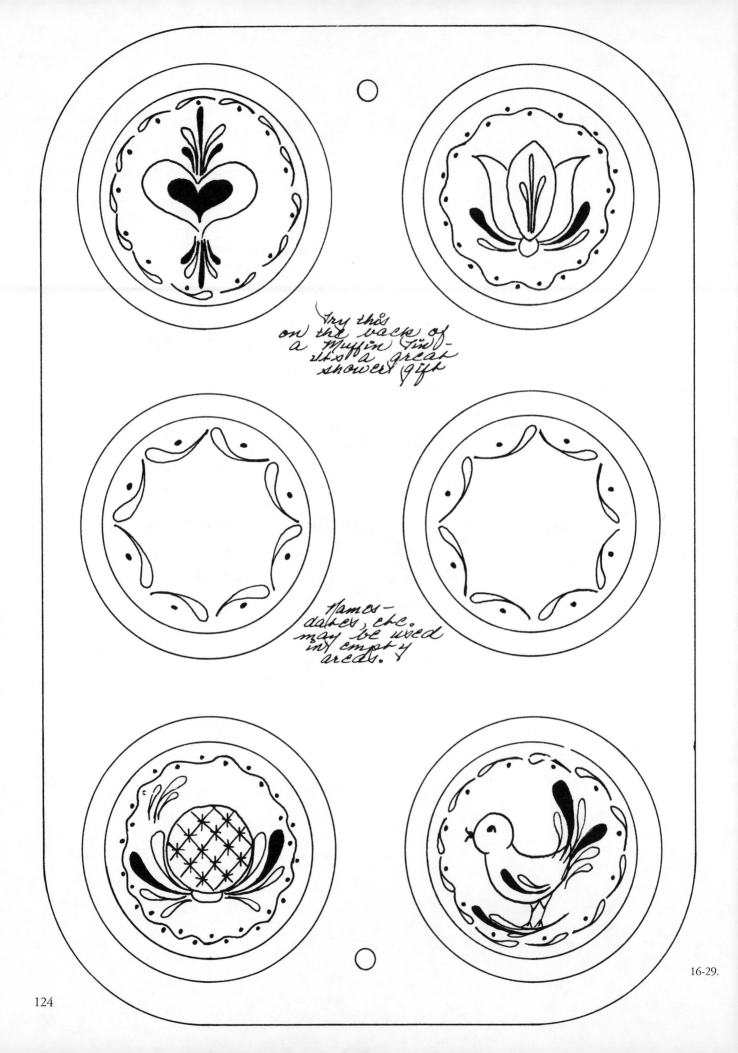

try this
on the back of
a Muffin Tin -
its a great
shower gift

names -
dates, etc.
may be used
in empty
areas. ↓

16-29.

16-30.

125

Designed for
a little Kyole
tray -- pattern
is versatile
and may
be used
in many
ways.

16-31.

126

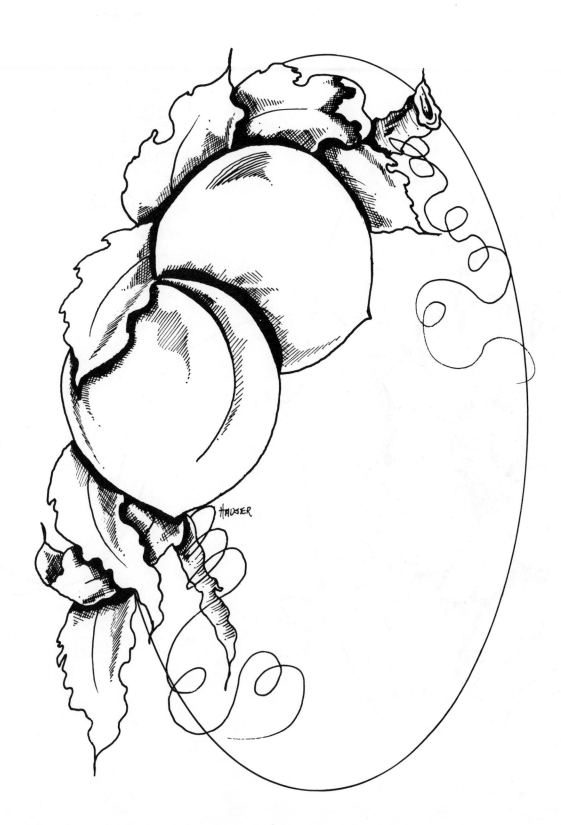

16-32.

16-33.

16-34.

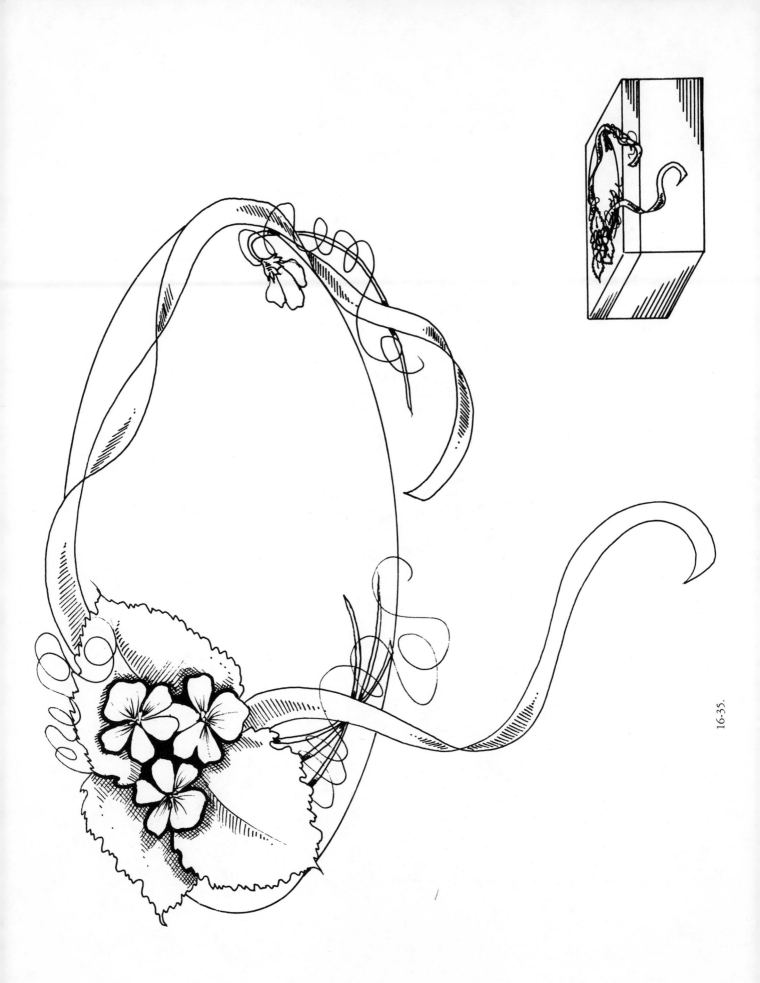

16-35.

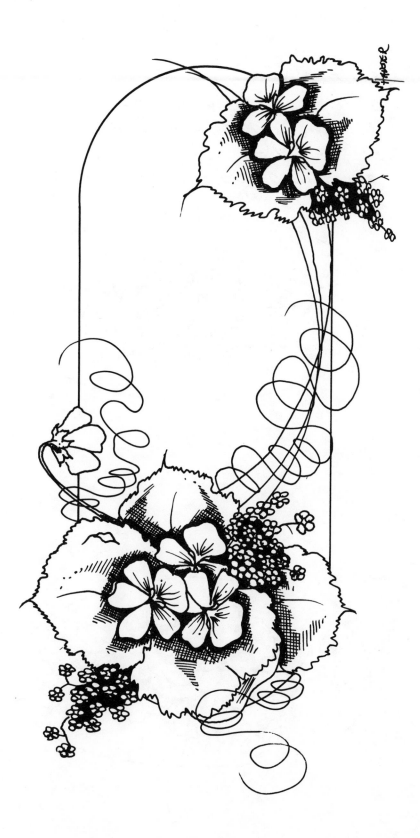

16-36.

Try these little designs
on the top of bars of soap –
or porcelain eggs – or even
candles — — — it's more fun — — —
than any thing you've ever done.

16-37.

16-38.

Try this basic rose design on a wooden hanger. It makes a charming bridal shower gift. This design lends itself well to a top desk or small stool or even a little girls dresser.

16-39.

134

Both these little patterns are good "first time" patterns.

16-40.

Roses take
practice - but
are worth
every minute
of it.

16-41.

16-42.

137

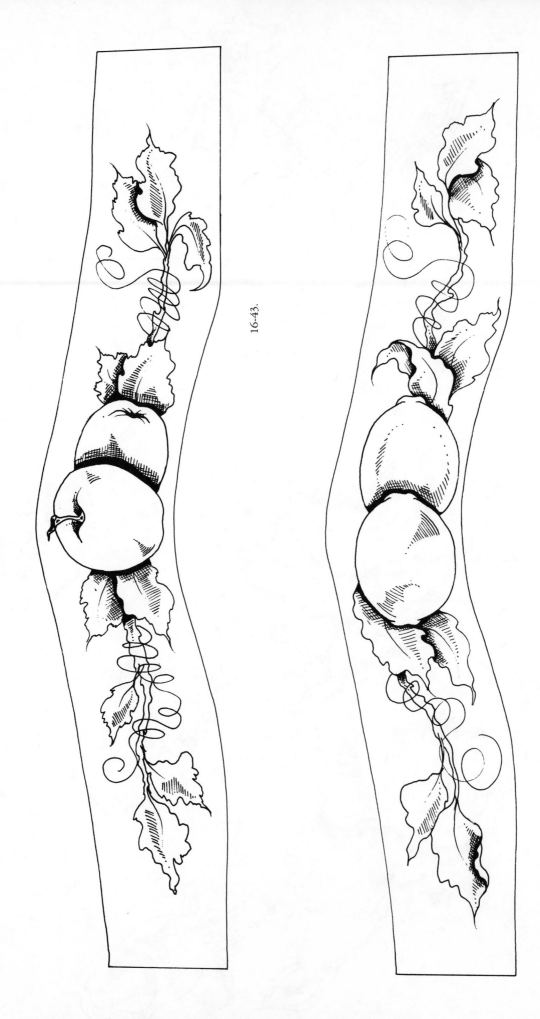

16-43.

16-44.

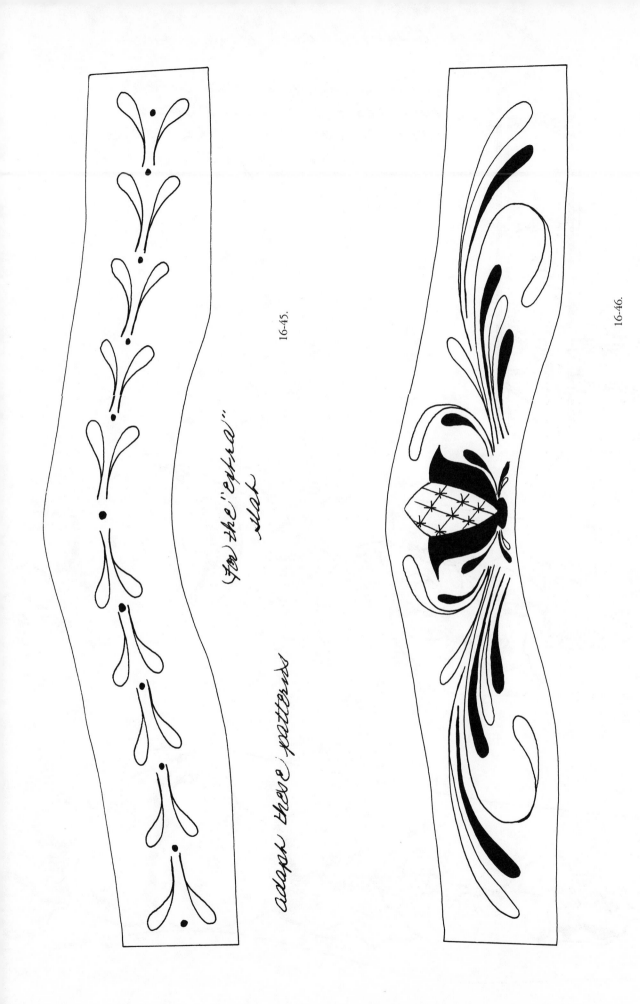

16-45.

16-46.

(for the "extra" slat

adapt these patterns

Ladder Back Chair Designs

The slats of ladder back chairs come in many shapes—however you may easily adapt these patterns to fit any of them.

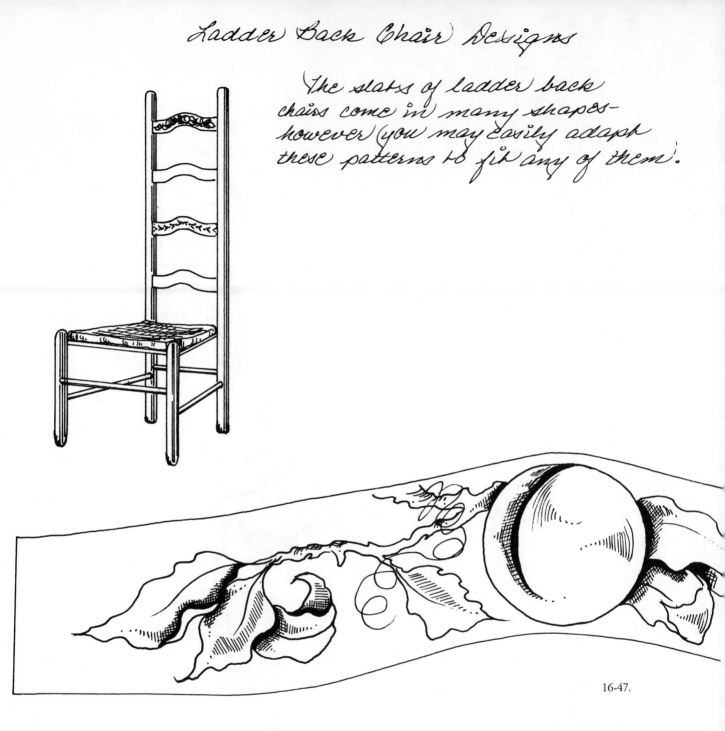

16-47.

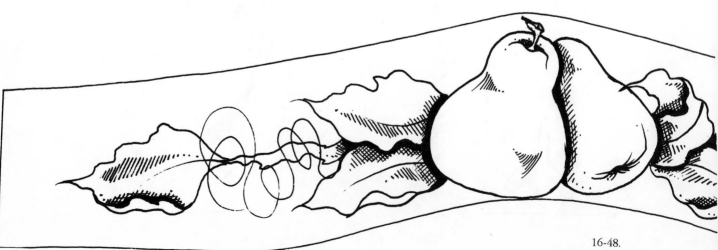

16-48.

*It's really neat to enlarge
these designs and use them on
drawers and other furniture.*

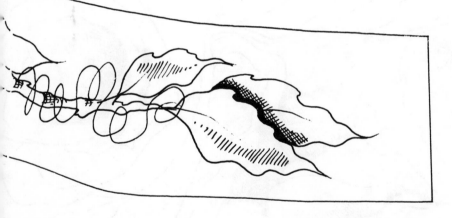

CoNNect Pattern LiNes

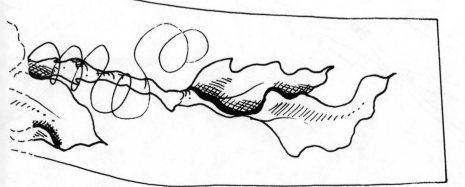

This design in whole - or in parts
would be lovely on an antique
trunk.

16-49.

Connect Pattern Lines

16-50.

143

This is wonderful on a Milk Can or Tavern Sign or just painted on an old barn wood board.

16-51.

144

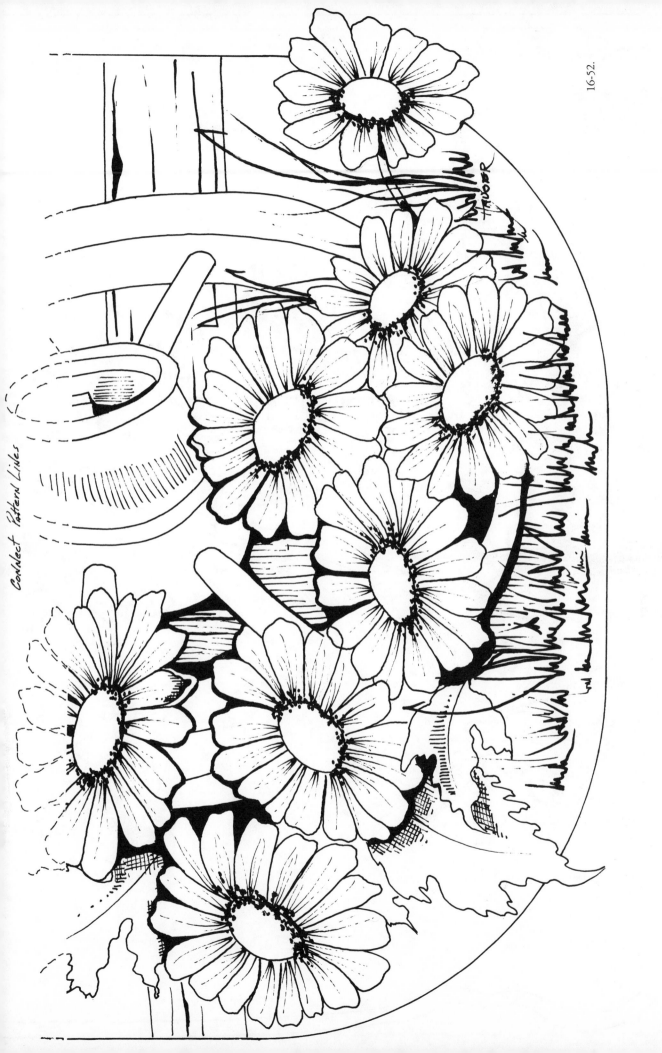

Connect Pattern Lines

16-52.

145

Lap Desk

Use india ink and
ink in scene in detail.
Color wash scene if desired.
or
Try this on an old Milk Can
—darling!

16-53.

146

Connect Pattern Lines

16-54.

Samples

CoNNect PatterN LiNes

16-56.

16-57

Priscilla Hauser Accredited Teachers and National Representatives

Priscilla's National Teaching Staff

Noreen Banes
2707 Albert
Carrollton, Texas 75077

Debby Boss
9705 S. 235th E. Avenue
Broken Arrow, Oklahoma 74012

Helen Hickish
2250 Old Nadeau Road
Palmdale, California 93550

Phyllis Lynn
94205 187th E. Avenue
Broken Arrow, Oklahoma 74012

Phillip Myer
St. James House #902 13th & Walnut Sts.
Philadelphia, Pennsylvania 19107

Linda Rudisill
5312 East 5th Street
Tulsa, Oklahoma 74112

Joyce Beebe
8505 Jade Acres Drive
Pensacola, Florida 32506

Betty Denton
29 Waynel Circle
Ft. Walton Beach, Florida 32548

Donna Johnson
12725 E. 137th Street South
Broken Arrow, Oklahoma 74012

Chris Myer
1429 East 38th Street
Tulsa, Oklahoma 74105

Beverly Page
771 So. Longwood Circle
Panama City, Florida 32405

Jeanne Serpa
31 Johnson Avenue
Narrogansette, Rhode Island 02882

Priscilla Hauser National Representatives

Alabama
Jolene Anderson, 318 Coffee Avenue N.E., Russelville 35653
Genie Amberson, 3525 Mill Run Road, Birmingham 35223
Jean Beckstrom, Route 1, Box 134A, Equality 36026
Jackie Burt, 505 Vincent Road S.E., Huntsville 35804
Carolyn Camp, Route 4, Box 251K, Athens 35611
Carolyn Collier, Athens Plaza, Athens 35611
Tricia Dempsey, 2500 Willena Drive, Huntsville 35803
Jan Dukes, 1002 Oakbowery Road, Opelika 36801
Bob Embry, Northside Mall, Ross Clark Circle, N.W., Dothan 36301
Debra Franklin, 1808 Opelika Road, Phenix City 36867
Jo S. Glenn, 317 Gunter Avenue, Wetampka 36092
Shirley Harris, Route 4, Box 365A, Madison 35738
Ponselle Haynes, Box 224, Route 1, River View 36872
Lynn Johnson, 430 Palisade, Florence 35630
Helen Johnston, 202 Wind Creek Way, Enterprise 36330
Herbie King, 505 Ardmore Lane, Birmingham 35210
Mary Ann Lemmond, 601 Main Street, Hartselle 35640

Mary Louise Radder, 2509 Robin Hood Dr., Mobile 36605
Mae Rainer, 410 Randwick Road, Dothan 36301
Gerry Rowe, 3335B Old Montgomery Highway, Birmingham 35202
Kay Ryan, 3631 Rainbow Drive, Tuscaloosa 35401
Mary Ann Scott, 1407 Scott Street, Opelika 36801
Arlene Sima, 1045 Hartford, Dothan 36301
Nancy Simpson, 1029 Antietam Road S.E., Huntsville 35803
JoAnn Walker, 314 Hillcrest Court, Opelika 36801
Lyda Wallace, 2811 19th Place South, Birmingham 35202
Hazel Ward, Star Route, Double Springs 35553
Mary A. Weeks, P.O. Box 305, Hamilton 35570
Linda Young, Route 5, Box 155, Bob Jones Avenue, Scottsboro 35768

Alaska
Sandi Herhold, P.O. Box 4544, Mount Edgecumbe 99835
Virginia Smith, 1020 G., Anchorage 99503

Arizona
Joyce Barnette, 11601 N. 66th Street, Scottsdale 85254
Penny Cantley, 8743 E. San Miguel, Scottsdale 85252
Mickey Castillo, 514 Morris, Mesa 85201

Emma Celeskey, 2855 N. Lane, Phoenix 85028
June Ehlers, 606 East 17th Street, Tucson 85711
Donna England, 2407 E. Dahlia, Phoenix 85001
Audrey Farrell, 445 N. 96th Place, Mesa 85207
Anna Jeanne Fox, 7783 Via Qonrisa, Scottsdale 85258
Ellen French, Route 1, Box 167, Somerton 85350
Marti Harnisch, 1167 E. Commonwealth, Chandler 85224
Rita Karls, 4301 N. 63rd Drive, Phoenix 85033
Letia H. Kerlee, 732 S. Penrose Circle, Mesa 85206
Ann Koch, Drawer T, 305 E. 5th Street, Benson 85206
Virginia Littlefield, 6730 Calle Padre, Tucson 85701
Ann Litzler, 67 Pine Ridge Drive, Flagstaff 86001
Diane Ponitch, 7402 E. Cortez, Scottsdale 85260
Margie Myers, 3010 W. Lisbon Court, Phoenix 85001
Dorothy Schafer, 8752 E. Hubbel, Scottsdale 85727
Naoma Tyner, 66 Pine Ridge Drive, Flagstaff 86001

Arkansas
Virginia Ashley, Box 789, Marianna 73260
* Pat Carter, Route 4, Kingsberry Estates, Mountain Home 72653

151

Betty Coger, Route 6, Huntsville 72740

Lynette Collums, Route 1, Bee Branch 72013

Margarite Fleming, 2324 E. Matthews, Jonesboro 72401

Gwen Flemister, 1532 Crestwood, North Little Rock 72116

Margurite Foster, 4200 Idlewild Avenue, North Little Rock 72116

Robin Hawkins, Route 7, Box 207, Mountain Home 72653

Merilynn Z. Johnson, 1302 State Line, Texarkana 75502

Ruth Johnson, 706 Pecan, Crosset 71635

Carol King, 1400 Old Forge, Apt. 1704, Little Rock 72207

Brenda Lincoln, 610 Fernwood, Benton 72015

Jennepher Marshall, 3001 Wedington, Fayetteville 72701

Mollie B. Phillips, 1816 Independence, Conway 73032

Betty Rothwell, R.R. 3, Quitman 72131

Mary Jane Todd, 4525 Park Avenue, Fort Smith 72901

Shirley C. Vaughan, Box 371, Morrilton 72110

Barbara Winemiller, 156 E. Cloverdale, Brinkley 72071

Betty Womack, 503 Newcomb Drive, Benton 72015

California

Delsa Allen, P.O. Box 1251, Yucca Valley 92284

Beth Atchison, 4297 Ridge Drive, Pittsburg 94565

Carol Jean Baker, 12327 DeSanda Avenue, Saratoga 95070

Llwellyn Baker, 19580 Penzance Street, Salinas 93901

Marie Bates, 577 Clarinada, Apt. 8, Daly City 94017

Barbara Benett, P.O. Box 745, Main Street, Diamond Springs 95619

Patti Bergin, 1171 Nimitz Lane, Foster City 94404

Arlete L. Bishop, 5365 Silver Reff Drive, Fremont 94538

Kathryn Bonfiglio, 2891 Benjamin Avenue, San Jose 95124

Jean Brown, 369 Birchwood Street, Modesto 95350

Diane B. Burtsfield, 2938 Carmel Way, Fairfield 94533

Kay Butcher, 1663 Tierra Montanosa, Alpine 92001

Doris Carlson, 9 Aloha Drive, Pacific Palisades 90272

Marlene Carr, 2388 Creekwood Court, Santa Rosa 95405

Joanne Cenicola, 7032 Via Serena, San Jose 94139

Etta F. Chinn, 190 Kimberlin Heights Dr., Oakland 94919

Marty Clay, 13252 Aubray, Poway 92064

Rena Louise Costa, 21601 E. Copperopolis Road, Linden 95214

Alice Coughlin, 2847 Wentworth, Shingle Springs 95214

Marolyn A. Currier, 18522 Chaparral Dr., Penn Valley 95977

Joan Dahl, 1564 Copenhagen Drive, Solvang 93463

Alice Deetz, Route 1, Box 565, Mt. Shasta 96067

Vicki Dietz, No. 83 Orange Blossom, Irvine 92664

A. Bernice Dolman, 2721 Los Amigos Ranch, Cordora 95670

Elizabeth Doran, 5712 Judith Street, San Jose 95123

Dorothy Dow, 719 Valle Vista, Vallejo 94590

Lou Edwards, Star Route 4, Pioneer 95666

Jean Fowler, 1224 Solano Avenue, Vallejo 94590

Lodema Gartman, 4504 N. Ventura Avenue, Ventura 93001

Dianne George, 1986 Winston Drive, Fairfield 94533

Selma George, 311 West Center Street, Yreka 96067

Sandra Gillespie, Route 3, Box 192H, San Luis Obispo 93401

Lee Gomez, 163 Mateo Street, San Leandro 94578

Laura Lynn Graham, 3567 Stallion Drive, Santa Rosa 95404

Diana L. Hackett, P.O. Box 7379, Tahoe City 95730

Winona Hanson, 2270 Wisconsin Ave, Redding 96001

Tracey Harrison, 14591 Bowling Green, Westminster 92683

Helen Hickish, 2250 Old Nadeau Road, Palmdale 93550

Mary Hogarth, 8605 Seventh Street, Downey 90241

Sandy Howell, 816 Marian Street, Vallejo 94590

Dorothy Ishimatsu, 5167 Country Lane, San Jose 95129

H. Haden Jordan, 168 Virginia Street, Haywood 94544

Carol Kimmel, 3035 Dersch Road, Anderson 96007

Jean Kistner, 5392 Hilltop Crestant, Oakland 94618

Ingrid Knudson, 2717 Del Amo Boulevard, Lakewood 90713

Oran Knudson, 2717 Del Amo Boulevard, Lakewood 90713

Ella Kulczewski, P.O. Box 131, Monte Rio 94014

Ellen Lipp, 35 Lighthouse Lane, Daly City 94014

Mickey Lynch, 2921 Sherwood Drive, San Carlos 94070

Louise McKenna, 2 Kimmie Court, Belmont 94002

Virginia Taft Meeks, 2055 Concord Blvd., Concord 94520

Lynn Gene Merrick, 3111 S.F. Street, Oxnard 93030

Barbara Neilsen, 1259 Bedford Street, Fremont 94538

Yukie Ohara, 932 September Drive, Cupertino 95014

Kristen Osgood, 1530 Pamela Crest, Redlands 92373

Cherlene Ostien, 1410 Ridley Avenue, Hacienda Heights, 91745

Cheryl Palmer, 19280 Valkenberg Lane, Auburn 95603

Jane Palmer, 2428 Lancaster Court, Hayward 94542

Bobbie Lee Pellerin, 6146 Etiwanda, Mira Loma 97752

Marlene Quitney, 1510 Hillcrest Road, Hollister 94023

Gloria Schneider, P.O. Box 568, Lower Lake 95457

Diana Silva, P.O. Box K, Sunol 94586

Frances E. Silva, Route 2, Box 249 M, Orland 95963

Gerry L. Silva, Star Route 1, Box 300, Etna 96027

Linda Smithson, 455 Berkshire Drive, Dixon 95620

Charlene Stempel, 2707 Michael Drive, Newbury Park 91320

Lavola Stock, 1886 S. Chester, Bakersfield 93302

Diane Strohmeyer, 1105 I Street, Petulama 94952

Lonnie L. Sutter, 1444 Key View, Corona Del Mar 92652

Clair Torrey, 5819 Morage Avenue, Oakland 94611

Pearl Tudor, 59 E. Lewis Street, Ventura 93001

Kathy Turner, 2292 Newquist Ct., Camarillo 93010

Katherine Valentine, 2302 Redondo Beach Boulevard, Torrance 90504

Joyce N. Van Vleet, 4602 Terrance Avenue, Oxnard 93030

Florence M. Wheeler, 10840 Aqueduct, Granada Hills 91344

Mary Whitney, 12277 Orizaba Avenue, Downey 90242

Ruth Ann Wise, 1609 Mt. Vernon Drive, Modesto 95350

Nancy Ann Yartz, 25372 Adelanto, Laguana Niguel 92677

Debbie Young, 2820 Tenaya Drive, Merced 95340

Rhae Young, 2820 Tenaya Drive, Merced 95340

Colorado

Beverly Barnett, 6574 South Balsam Ct., Littleton 80123

Judy Bell, 7660 East Cedar Avenue, Denver 80231

Jeanne Benzie, 2018 Prong Horn Lane, Colorado Springs 80915

Sheryle Bonnell, 632 N. 15th Street, Grand Junction 81501

Lois Brady, 1265 Olathe Street, Aurora 80011

Ellen Carlson, 1608 Heber Drive, Ft. Collins 80521

Sr. Mary Imelda Cox, Route 3, Box 75 Golden 80401

Linda Dickerson, 8965 Yukon Street, Westminster 80020

Cathy Erickson, 3550 S. Kendall 1-203, Denver 80235

Velma Habiger, 3212 Carson Street, Evans 80620

Vivian Houghtling, 118 Adams, Monte Vista 81144

Donna Johnson, 235 Flora Way, Golden 80401

Patti Kraus, 2713 S. Meade, Denver 80236

Jean Mackay, 3680 Ames Street, Denver 80212

Alberta M. Murray, 13149 W. Ohio Avenue, Denver 80226

Eileene Pippinger, 7447 S. Lamar, Littleton 80123

Barbara Reese, 1854 Frontier Road, Greeley 80631

Judy Richards, 5108 S. Nelson, Denver 80123

Marjorie Richardson, 2359 Monument Drive, Grand Junction 81503

Betty Sours, 5153 S. Miller Street, Littleton 80123

Jeanne Spencer, 35523 Weld Co. Rd 31, Eaton 80615

Karrel Stevens, 3510 Inspiration, Colorado Springs 80917

Dorothy Thorngren, 5170 E. Asbury, Denver 80222

Alberta Teasley, 5215 Kendrick Court, Golden 80401

Connecticut

Sonya Bird, 775 Manchester Road, Glastonbury 06033

JoAnn Braun, 254 Fairfield Woods Road, Fairfield 06430

Georgia Ferris, 87 Fulling Mill Lane, Ridgefield 06430

Doreen Gammons, 13 Robin Lane, Killingworth 06417

Ruth Ann Greenhill, 51 Platt Lane, Mildord 06460

Bertha Guay, Box 111, Route 19, Stafford 06075

Jean Hansen, Pettipaug Road, Box 835, R.R.2, Westbrook 06498

Esther Hoffman, 184 Rosemere Avenue, Fairfield 06432

Marie LeFeyre, 20 Millbrook Road, Stamford 06902

Deanne Pape, 422 Main Street, Old Saybrook 06475

Joan T. Wadleigh, 15 Oakwood Drive, Gales Ferry 06335

Florida

Barbara Anderson, 12135 S. Dixie, Miami 33156

Jean Archer, 7109 Lauder Place, Tampa 33617

Cheryl Arthur, 2610 Citrus Blvd, Haines City 33814

Shirley Baad, 175 Indiana Mound Trail, Tavernier 33070

Estelle Barley, 470 Ninth Street, North Naples 33940

Joyce Beebe, Route 7, Box 402-D, Pensacola 32506

Rita Bohn, 2241 Amhurst, Lynn Haven 32444

Pati Bondi, Route 7, Box 402-H, Pensacola 32506

Joyce Brantley, 254 Bayshore Road, Gulf Breeze 32561

Jane Brown, General Delivery, Ponce de Leon 32461

Pat Burdick, 404 E. Church, Dade City 33525

Jane Burkett, 18925 S. W. 248 Street, Homestead 33033

Patricia Butler, 7 N.E. 17th Avenue, Pompano Beach 33060

Linda Calderon, 307 17th Street, Niceville 32578

Nan Champion, 831 Indian Trail, Destin 32541

Vickie Cole, 432 Gregory Avenue, Valporaiso 32580

Christine Colley, 2808 E. Strong, Pensacola 32504

B. J. Cook, 4032 C. W. Kennedy, Tampa 33609

Sally Croft, Route 2, Box 107–L, Crystal River 32629

Jan Cross, 141 John Sims Parkway, Niceville 32578

Brita Darling, 3025 Huntington Drive, Tallahassee 32303

Betty Denton, 29 Waynel Circle, Ft. Walton Beach, 32548

Lucille S. Dickinson, 15805 S. W. 242 St., Homestead 33031

Julie Dillinger, 701 Overbrook Drive, Ft. Walton Beach 32548

Martha Frenzel, 4617 St. Nazaire Road, Pensacola 32505

Margaret Gay, 1918 Wilson Avenue, Panama City 32405

Nell Gerry, 3303 Hopkins, Titasville 31780

Dorothy Hermsdorfer, 107 Chelsea House, Port Charlotte 33952

Ruth Herman, 6705 N.W. 169th Street, Apt. C110, Hialeah 33015

Fay Herrington, 2581 Telstar Avenue, Orlando 32805

Dee Hesington, 1400 Lakeview Avenue, Eustis 32726

Margaret Hofsetter, 8325 S.E. 116 Terr., Miami 33156

Ginny Holtgreven, 1013 Tarpon Drive, Treasure Island 33740

Andy Jones, Route 3, Box 629, Tallahassee 32308

Ann Jones, Route 3, Box 629, Tallahassee 32308

Mary Ann Katch, 4822 S.W. 1st Ct., Cape Coral 33904

Wanda Lear, 617 Briarwood Road, Venice 33595

Barbara Lobsinger, 5600 Turbin Street, Orlando 32807

Dorothy Luscombe, 3423 E. Silver Springs Boulevard, Ocala 32670

Peggy Maudlin, 2268 N.W. 30th Road, Boca Raton 33431

Carole McCully, 5631 St. Amatus Road, Pensacola 32503

Marsha McDowell, 16 Villa Drive, Okeechobee 33472

Martha McLean, 1166 S. Patrick No. 1, Satellite Beach 32937

Doris Merritt, P.O. Box 192, Lynn Haven 32444

Beverly Page, 771 So. Longwood Circle, Panama City 32405

Sue M. Peacock, 2220 N.W. 55 Blvd. No. 35, Gainesville 32601

Linda Price, 8225 Fachom Road, Pensacola 32504

Marilyn Rector, 260 Gulf Terrace, Destin 32541

Verna E. Reich, 5200 N.E. 5th Avenue, Ft. Lauderdale 33334

Judy Rouse, 22 James Avenue, Shalimar 32579

Mary M. Seeman, 7402 Lake Breeze Drive S.W., Apt 212, Ft. Myers 33907

Leah A. Smith, 4737 Baywood Drive, Lynn Haven 32444

Darlene Snyder, 1233 S.E. 10th Avenue, Ocala 32670

Hazel Stills, 1216 West Vine Street, Kissimmee 32741

Vera Stuckey, 800 Firestone Way, New Port Richey 33535

Sally Stone, 615 E. Silver Springs, Ocala 32670

Pug Swain, 131 Alabama Avenue, Brooksville 33512

Glenda C. Thomas, Route 2, Box 316, Crystal River 32629

Jackie Thumser, 152 Point O'Woods Dr., Daytona Beach 32014

Carolyn Waldrop, 5216 Firestone Road, Jacksonville 32210

Jerrye Winters, 2036 San Marino Ways, Clearwater, 33515

Kathy Whiteside, 95 S.E. 7th Avenue, Deerfield Beach 33441

Dorothy Wood, 5027 Dorlan Avenue, Orlando 32809

Pam Ziemba, 5450 Hansel Avenue, Orlando 32809

Georgia

Wayne Adams, Box 22, Hoschton 30548

Hilda Akins, Route 1, Chula 31733

Anne Barker, 1477 Gloria Street, Griffin 30223

Louise C. Brown, Rockmart Road, Route 1, Cartersville 30120

Mary D. Bruner, Box 705, Blakely 31723

Carroll Byers, 1943 Queens Way, Chamblee 30341

Elaine Chord, 8740 Roswell Road N.E., Atlanta 30338

Addie Davis, 889 Wimbish Road, Macon 31208

Barbara Geer, 2617 Langland Ct., N.E., Atlanta 30345

Carol Harris, P.O. Box 626, Valdosta 31601

Judith M. Harvey, 738 Beechwood Drive, Savannah 31406

Yolanda Heiss, 5254 Memorial Drive, Stone Mountain 30083

Tammy Horney, Route 2, Gainesville 30501

Joyce McClure, P.O. Box 273, Pearl Street, Shellman 31786

Ruth Murphy, 1670 Debbie Drive, Marbleton 33059

Sylvia V. Novack, 5248 Smokerise Drive, Stone Mountain 30083

June Pendley, P.O. Box 56, Chula 31733

Nancy Stepler P.O. Box 683, Blakely 31723

Ronnie Tinnerman, 2219 Plymouth, Maretta 30062

Linda Williford, 408 S. Jefferson, Ashburn 31714

Hawaii

Lora Anderson, 500 University Avenue, Apt. 1414, Honolulu 96814

Rae Marie Copeland, 204 Third Street, Honolulu 96818

Barbara Del Piano, 471 Kapuhube Avenue, Honolulu 96815

Gini McCormick, 333 Uly Niu Street, Kailua 96734

Idaho

Sharon DeGarimore, Box 772, McCall 83638

Bertha Fullmer, 236 S. 1st West, Resburg 83440

Glena Greiner, 534 West 17th, Burley 83318

Carol J. King, 815 S. Holmes, Idaho Falls 83401

Dottie Nester, Route 4, Box 4067, Burley 83318

Muriel Worthylake, Star Route, Box 290, McCammon 83250

Illinois

Dorris J. Alm, 1319 W. Concord Lane, Schaumburg 60193

Sandra Aubuchon, 905 N. Cleveland, E. Effingham 62401

Eloise Baxter, 135 E. Madison, Rushville 62681

Chris Bernstein, 2001 E. Washington Street, Bloomington 61701

Roberta Blick, 18 N. 7th Avenue, St. Charles 60174

Cynthia Borman, 522 Tanglewood Lane, Frankfort 60423

Toni Carbo, 1400 W. 55th Place, Countryside 60525

Betty Cathcart, 320 South Park, Maressa 62257

Harlene Childres, 562 N. Van Nortwick, Batavia 60510

Bobbie Cox, 106 Gum Street, Harrisburg 62946

Ann Cunningham, 502 S. Vale, Bloomington 61701

Joyce Davis, Route 1, Box 64, Seneca 61360

Paula Devore, 112 N. 3, P.O. Box 304, Altamont 62411

Jane Dobbs, Route 5, Salem Road, Mt. Vernon 62864

Ardith Dolamore, 146 W. LeMoyne, Lombard 60148

Bonnie Doty, Route 2, Princeton 61356

Martha Durant, R.R. 2 Box 124, Martinsville 62442

Donna Fahlgren, 904 N. Laporte, Melrose Park 60161

Angee Fikaris, 160 Burlington, Clarendon Hill 60514

Sammie Funderburk, 209 E. 14th Street, Naperville 60540

Agnes Gardner, 67 Beth Ann Drive, Belleville 62221

Karen Gehm, 2717 Seventh Street, Peru 61354

Opal L. Green, 3729 Ruth Drive, Granite City 62040

Mitzi Hands, 245 Roosevelt Road, West Chicago 60185

Patricia Harris, Route 3, Quincy 62301

Roberta M. Helson, 1 S. 609, Lorraine Glen Ellyn 60137

Grace Herr, 70 Eastgate Drive, Danville 61732

Winnie Heuer, 1750 Meadow Lane, Bannockburn 60015

Carol Hill, 1704 W. Gilbert Avenue, Peoria 61604

Linda R. Hoelter, 100 East St. Paul Street, Spring Valley 61362

Shirley Hollingsworth, 511 So. Chicago Avenue, Bismarck 61814

Delores Klippert, 1003 N. Fernandez, Arlington Heights 60004

Elsie R. Kelm, 7631 Monroe Street, Forest Park 60130

Sharon Knight, 238 S. Richmond, Westmount 60559

Peggy Legeriet, 1819 Neville Street, Metropolis 62960

Karen Machino, 1704 Venice Avenue, Granite City 62040

Sharon McGlasson, 1928 8th Street, Peru 61354

Sharon Middleton, 4107 Dean Drive, Decatur 62526

Linda Miller, 317 Jana Road, Macomb 61455

Rita Miller, 1929 Weathersfield Way, Schaumburg 60193

Roberta Miller, 14901 S. Kostner Avenue, Midlothian 60445

Murriel Mills, 214 N. Dunton Avenue, Arlington Heights 60006

Doris Mook, 1252 State Drive, Alton 62002

Verna Morris, R.R. 1, Jacksonville 62650

Cathy Mrasak, R.R. 2, Rochester 62563

Phyllis Neff, 1162 Michelle Lane, Lombard 60148

Wilma Noe Payne, R.R. 1, Box 96A, Stewardson 62463

Sharon Pirro, 34 West Wilson, Lombard 60148

Erma Ragle, 4650 Fitzgerald Road, Decatur 62521

Anne Reynolds, 205 N. Border, Maressa 62257

Gina Richardson, 423 S. Cherry, Centralia 62801

Carolyn Routeledge, 1212 N. Logan, Danville 61832

Wanda Schmidt, 801 Ninth Street, Highland 63249

Harriet V. Schultz, 1818 Fairway Court, Kankakee 60901

Anne Seale, 603 Harris Avenue, Greenville 62246

Claudia Segmon, Route 1, Box 476-2, Westville 61883

Pat Werthe, 1119 Woodland Avenue, Batavia 60510

Ellen Wiesner, 8531 W. Cermack, North Riverside 60546

Marie Wilson, 1605 White Street, Mt. Vernon 62864

Indiana

Linda Albrecht, 1951 Berne Avenue, Terre Haute 47805

Wilma J. Amos, 804 E. Lanuack Road, Indianapolis 46220

Margaret Berlien, 120 E. Main, Brownsburg 46112

Sara Baumgardner, 5632 Radner Road, Indianapolis 46226

Midge Bond, 1260 W. 86th Street, Indianapolis 46206

Elva Borth, 90 E. College Avenue, Morocco 47963

Dianne Burrell, 1712 Shepherd Drive, Anderson 46011

Donna Campbell, 510 Main Street, Vincennes 47591

Maryhelen Carroll, 2924 E. Cameron Street, Indianapolis 46229

Elaine Cioni, 53 West 68th Place, Merrillville 46410

Cathy Cohen, Stanton Lake Lot 117, Leesburg 46538

Dawn R. Cornell, 1700 E. First Street A73, Anderson 46012

Barbara M. Dillon, 416 Main, Rockport 47635

Nancy J. Engledow, 11822 Lancaster Cir., Carmel 46032

Barbara Gephart, 7712 Main, Richmond 47374

Patricia Gray, 7453 Cotherstone Court, Indianapolis 46256

Pat Greer, South Plaza Building, Newburgh 47630

Maxine Hales, 922 E. Lincoln Drive, Mt. Vernon 47620

Ruth Harmon, 33 S. Washington, Danville 46122

Evelyn Kirsch, Box 128, Ambia 47917

Rosalie Landau, Route 1, Box 143, Muncie 47302

Shelley E. Martin, 1217 Liberty, Covington 47932

Roena Preston, 313 State Street, New Albany 47250

Karen Roberts, 6625 Finchley Road, Indianapolis 46206

Anne Roman, 7818 Delcon Drive, Fort Wayne 46801

Ida Russell, 740 Main Street, Brookville 47012

Mary Scanlon, 1772 E. 116, Carmel 46032

Lois J. Schell, 5648 E. Saugana, Rolling Prairie 46371

Suzie Schmitz, 6455 Kingswood Drive, Indianapolis 46206

Martha Searcy, 2714 Kaywood, New Albany 47150

Leona Shafer, 5606 Springlake Drive, Evansville 47710

Rosella Sisco, 61194 Locust Drive, South Bend 46624

Amy L. Stahl, 492 Manor Drive, Seymour 47274

Jessie Mae Walker, 408 Seymour Road, Crothersville 47227

Pat Walker, 2205 Hanover, Indianapolis 46227

Pam Wampler, Route 3, Ballywood, LaPorte 46350

Jean C. Weber, 1306 Bullseye Road, Valporaiso 46383

Sheila Wiles, 3007 Calumet Avenue, Valporaiso 46383

Carol Williams, 163 N. Main, Martinsville 46151

Iowa

Andrea Bean, Route 1, Albert City 50510

Audrey Bettin, R.R. 2, Odebolt 51458

Eileen Blaskovich, Lohrville 51453

Dorothy Boeckmann, 902 Second Avenue N.E., Waverly 50677

Kathryn Brandon, Box 144, Logan 51546

Maxine Citta, 2201 7th Street, Harlan 51537

Margaret Clayton, 2622 Beaver Avenue, Des Moines 50301

Janet Edgar, 1675 Kennedy Road, Dubuque, 52001

Bernice Fullhart, 303 Westwood Drive, Ames 50010

Donna Goode, 8383 University, Des Moines 50301

Katie Gorsuch, 701 Third Avenue S.E., Cedar Rapids 52406

Pat Hays, 717 Eighth Street, Boones 50036

Alleen Hedge, R.R. 1, Fremont 52561

Karen Horn, 28 Bohnker Hill Road, Denison 51442

Shirley Johnstone, 10 W. 4th, Spencer 51301

Mildred Karber, West Main, Grand Junction 50107

Trellis Kitt, R.R. 2, Sac City 50583

Sheryl Kuiper, R.R. 1, Archer 51231

Patricia Leddon, P.O. Box 87, Scarville 50473

Faye Lenz, R.R. 2, Wapello 52653

Marcella Nicol, 512 Cedar Bend, Waterloo 50703

Renee Nordyke, Middle 52307

Patti Ristau, 501 S.E. 6th Street, Ankony 50021

Emilie Schultz, Macrama Mill, Burlington 52601

Carol Stiers, 301 Kirkwood Avenue, Iowa City 52240

Vi Thurmond, 343 S.E. Miller, Des Moines 50301

Julie Van Cleave, R.R. 1, Perry 50220

Ruby Weber, Cedarcrest Road, Columbus Junction 52738

Joan White, Macrama Mill, Burlington 52601

Carol Whitters, Route 2, Cedar Rapids 52406

Louise Wiley, Route 2, Carlise 50047

Kansas

Joan Allen, 308 N. Sixth, Chetopa 67336

Carol Bennett, 8221 Crandview, Overland Park 66204

Lois Black, 546 W. Main, Valley Center 66088

Kay Campbell, 9316 W. 77 Terrace, Overland Park 66204

Margaret Carlson, 508 N. Kansas, Liberal 67901

Mary Channell, 1520 Center Street, Goodland 67735

Lucille Clark, 1003 Apache, Wichita 67202

Lois Cooper, 3401 Hillcrest Road, Independence 67301

Lois Cranor, 120 N. First Street, Independence 67301

Virginia Cranston, 9 Rambler Road, Hutchinson 67501

Jan Forsyth, 209 S. Walnut, Medicine Lodge 67104

Elsie J. Fox, 2045 N. 42nd Street, Kansas City 66104

Jerg Frogley, 502 Fifth, Oswego 67356

Beverly Goble, 1106 Neosho, Emporia 66802

Susan Ann Green, P.O. Box 8, Burns 66840

Lorraine Hadsell, 626 E. Main, Masion 66861

Mary Haltom, 14 East Second Street, Hutchinson 67501

Alice Higdon, 7612 Warren, Witchita 67201

Barbara House, 101 E. Northview, McPherson 67460

Lucy Moffitt, 1220 Taft, Great Bend 67530

Clara Murry, Box 606, 603 N. Eighth, Garden City 67846

Dane Normile, Denton 66017

Katherine Oltjen, R.R. 1, Everest 66424

Maxine Rauscher, P.O. Box 184, Goodland 67735

Carolyn Sayler, 1107 Harding, Garden City 67846

Eleanor Scott, 120 N. First Street, Independence 67301

Sandy Shields, 14 Century Parkway, Neodesha 66757

B. J. Smith, Box 280, Leoti 67861

Judith Steffen, 1221 W. 14th Street, Chanute 66720

Regina Tarwater, P.O. Box 302, St. Paul 66771

Connie Weibe, 602 West Fifth, Coffeyville 67337

Betty Wick, 313 A. Street, Abilene 67410

Kentucky

Leslie Allen, 3503 Sarah Lane, Bowling Green 42101

Mildred Bennett, Route 1, Eddyville 42038

Anna Lois Beumel, 2705 Morningside Drive, Owensboro 42301

Jo Crary, 70 Orchard Hill, Fort Thomas 41075

Rosemary Ewen, R.R. 3, Box 611, Hazard 41701

Jewel Dean Ford, P.O. Box 127, Greensburg 42743

Gayle Laible, 478 Kuhrs Lane, Covington 41012

Una Mayhew, 1428 Laurel Avenue, Bowling Green, 42101

Lessie Moreno, 232 Indiana Trail, Radcliffe 40160

Betty Muffett, Box 266 Main Street, Burnside 42519

Louise Shelton, 2901 Thistlewood Drive, Louisville 40206

Louisiana

Deena Blanchard, 200 Chastant Boulevard, Lafayette 70508

Eileen Cannon, 4365 Perkins Road, Baton Rouge 70808

Faye Drobnic, Box 427, Patterson 70392

Zella Duncan, 822 Shady Lane, Westlake 70669

Debbie Folse, 112 Barrios Street, Lockport 70374

Judy Folse, 112 Barrios Street, Lockport 70374

Delia Green, 309 N. Pierce, Metairie 70004

Shirley Grisham, Route 1, Box 265, Calhoun 71225

Myriam Harmon, 130 E. Randall Court, Gretna 70053

Marverine Hickman, 245 Brookwood, Alexandria 71301

Sandy Hogan, 3719 Greenway Place, Shreveport 71105

Barbara Houser, 8424 Ridgemont Drive, Pineville 71360

Janie Mistick, Box 314, Buras 70041

Leta Mock, Route 2, Box 63, Lecompte 71246

Emmylou Montgomery, 1201 W. Jefferson, Lake Charles 70601

Joyce Oldham, 1103 Rathburn, Minden 71055

Marilyn Oliver, 3603 Royce Drive, Alexandria 71303

Patricia Price, 303 Benville Street, Winnfield 71483

Gayle Bass Robinson, Route 2, Box 162, DeVille 71328

Betty S. Swearingen, 8739 Jefferson, Baton Rouge 70616

Judith Teague, 6039 Gaylyn Drive, Shreveport 71102

Polly Waldron, 2208 Briarmont Street, Monroe 71202

Connie White, 176 Oakwood, Mandeville 70448

Betty L. Woodhead, Box 517, Sterlington 71280

Maine

Mona W. Ridley, R.F.D. 1, Waldoboro 04572

Linda Whitney, 143 Water Street, Skowhegan 04976

Maryland

Nancy Clark, 220 Randolph Road, Silver Springs 20875

Linda E. Dickinson, 9305 Tuckerman Seabrook 20801

Linda B. Foote, 8510 Goodluck Road, Lanham 20801

Margaret E. Glass, 7617 Carteret Road, Bethesda 20034

Marilyn Knight, 12146 Long Ridge Lane, Bowie 20715

Leona Leland, Route 2, Box 36, Bluebird Court, Leonard 20650

Beverly Martin, 331 Wende Way, Glen Burnie 21061

Roberta P. Maushardt, 8204 Peach Orchard Road, Dundalk 21222

Helen Randles, 15321 Narcisus Way, Rockville 20853

Marilynne Roberson, 17440 Naylor Road, Sabillasville 21780

Iva C. Wessinger, 6807 Picnic Woods Road, Middletown 21769

Massachusetts

Judy Arsenault, 339 Chestnut, Gardner 02440

Nancy Bock, 63 Wenham Road, Topsfield 01983

Claire S. Casperson, 1 Indian Hill Road, Burlington 01803

Ginny Dandreta, 177 Swan Street, Methuen 01844

Joyce Dipasquale, 1 Gladwalt Road, Northboro 01532

Joanne Dzengielewski, 30 Washburn Street, Dorchester 02125

Ethel Hannabury, 129 Porter Street, Melrose 02176

Dorothy M. Johnson, 176 Hunt Road, Chelmsford 01824

Maya Johnson, 116 Gateway Drive, Springfield 01119

Julie Kelly, 88 River Road, Norfolk 02056

Vellis King, 13 Spring Street, North Brookfield 01535

Madeleine Lucier, 54 Wilson Street, Spencer 01562

Carol Ann McGrath, 2 Fountain Street, Billerica 01821

Gene Mahoney, 1166 Main Street, Hungham 02034

Helen A. Owens, 390 Southbridge Street, Auburn 01501

Jean Reader, 12 The Great Road, Bedford 02730

Marilyn Rich, Weathers Lane, Bolton 01470

Katherine Ryan, 191 Westwood Avenue, East Long 01028

Bette St. Martin, 397 Main, Fitchburg 01420

Pat Sasanecki, 50 Brookside Drive, Wilbraham 01095

Alice Smith, 523 M. Westfield, Feeding Hill 01030

Joan Sprague, 491 Prospect Street, Longmeadow 01028

Patricia A. Tanguay, 24 Ashland Avenue, Methuen, 01844

Marianne Trepanier, 308 Moss Avenue, North Andover 01845

Katharine Turnblom, 100 Greenwood, Worcester 01607

Constance M. Turner, 37 Washington Street, Reading 01867

Suzanne Weise, 6 Whittier Road, Milford 01757

Muriel Woodruff, 76 Orange Street, Reading 01867

Lorraine Wrenn, 29 Crabtree Road, Plymouth 02360

Michigan

Lynda Akins, 244 E. Washington, Coldwater 49036

Doris Austin, Route 2, 62 Street, Hartford 49087

Jean G. Barlett, 103 E. Colby Street, Whitehall 49461

Suzanne C. Bouchard, 1875 Camille Drive S.E., Grand Rapids 49506

Ardath Burry, 931 Vine Street, Adrian 49221

Pat DeGraw, 224 Michael Avenue, Shepherd 48883

Doris Dickson, 39649 Moravian Drive, Mt. Clemens 48043

Kerry Dorstewitz, Route Box 451, Waterbil 49098

Merlyn Duisterhot, 426 E. Michigan, Kalamazoo 49003

Mary L. Ellis, 5385 Pointe Drive, Marine City 48039

Thelma Erway, 11031 Hastings Point Road, Middleville 49333

Gloria Fedoruk, 17144 Englewood, Allen Park 48101

Marie Fowler, 9550 S. Luce, Perrinton 48871

Sue Garner, 504 Ojwba, Oscoda 48750

Roberta Goupil, Route 2, Box 512A, Houghton Lake 48629

Jean L. Guenther, 1424 Birchrest Drive, Dearborn 48124

Betsy Ann Hill, 1033 107th Avenue, Plainwell 49080

Dorothy Johnson, 6851 Rosemary, Dearborn Heights 48127

Marie Kimsey, 2715 N. Fifth Street, Kalamazoo 49009

Carrie Kirshaman, 1604 Main West, Kalamazoo 49002

Florence Lossing, Box 24, St. Clair 48079

Cynthia L. Lowrie, 2923 Cooper Avenue, Port Huron 49060

Patricia Mifsud, 111 Brentwood, Dearborn 48124

Linda Miller, 1335 E. Grand River, Portland 48875

Patricia Petro, 11523 E. Bath Road, Byron 48418

Mary Lou Raftery, 1127 U.S. 31, P.O. Box 254, Petoskey 49770

Joyce E. Richter, 4801 S. Cedar, Lansing 48910

Elizabeth Roush, 2313 Pierce Street, Flint 48503

Jackie Sanderson, 52 E. Jefferson, Quincy 49082

Judy Schneider, 201 N. Riverside, St. Clair 48079

Pat Seay, 605 Adrian Street, Tecumseh 49286

Priscilla Shaffner, 19500 Hilton, Southfield 48075

Marge Skrobot, 391 Midlakes Boulevard, Plainwell 49080

Velda Jean Smith, 1482 Cahour Road, Addison 49220

Sharon Stoeckel, 1496 Rosyln Road, Grosse Point Woods 48236

Pat Szukhent, 913 Birchwood Drive, Flushing 48433

Rosalie Szukhent, 7044 Elmo Road, Flushing 48433

Dori Towsley, 37 Patricia Drive, Coldwater 49036

Susan Van Tuyl, 303 Smith Street, No. 305, Clio 48420

Jo Veccellio, 1510 Country Club Drive, Niles 49120

Lynette B. Wells, 1005 Carlton Boulevard, Jackson 49201

Betty Wichman, 9980 N. Tittawaw Assee, Freeland 49623

Elouise "Pud" Wilson, 406 Park Avenue, Yale 48097

Minnesota

Rita Kay Bakke, 900 S. Second, Marshall 56258

Marian Bestor, P.O. Box 303, Rochester 55960

Charlene Brose, 11566 Bailey, Woodburg 55055

Karen Clarke, 7038 Angus Avenue, Inver Grove Heights 55076

C. Joyce Cody, 109 Howard Street, Hibbing 55746

Eileen D. Conrow, 3302 Kentwood G, Burnsville 55337

Donna Gould, 815 S. 10th Street, Moorehead 56560

Norma Hallisey, R.R. 6, Box 75, Fergus Falls 56537

Helen Halstead, Route 2, Box 150, Brooten 56316

Florence Hasbargen, R.R. 3, Jewitt Lake, Fergus Falls 56537

Joyce Morsching, P.O. Box 73, Newport 55055

Shirley Olsen, 1425 Eighth Avenue North, St. Cloud 56301

Barbara Otto, Box 295, Atkin 56431

Kay Portz, 814 N. Grace Street, St. Peters 56082

Linda Quist, 14-4th Avenue S.E., Elbow Lake 56531

Mary Ralston, 720 S. Miller, Litchfield 55355

Barbara J. Smith, 911 W. Summit, Fergus Falls 56537

Joy Smith, Plaza Square Center, Thnonia 55987

Marabeth Timmers, 1621 E. Sandhurst Drive, St. Paul 55109

Dianne Verba, Route 2, Box 30, Sauk Center 56378

Sandra Walker, Box 118, Oronoco 55960

Ann Jackson Wright, 819 S.E. 9th Avenue, Faribault 55021

Mississippi

Barbara Allen, Route 3, Box 566, Gulfport 39503

Jo Anne Ashcraft, Box 1411, Greenwood 38930

Carolyn Boone, 215 Eastwood Drive, Columbus 39701

Sue Dees, 13 Kimball Drive, Gulfport 39501

Martha Edwards, 414 Wood Street, Water Valley 38965

Pat Harris, Route 1, Box 244, Tommsuba 39301

Gerri Hughes, 1214 Winterview Drive, Jackson 39204

Liz Lumpkin, 1750 Maria Drive, Jackson 39204

Bernadette M. Mabry, 703 Emerald Lane, Hattiesburg 39401

Edna Manley, 3420 55th Place, Meridian 39301

Barbara McBride, Route 1, Box 705, Florence 39073

Jane McWilliams, 2405 51st Avenue, Meridian 39301

Georgia Nagorka, Box 188, Lumberton 39445

Beckeye Robbins, Route 7, Box 393, Hattiesburg 39401

Mona Lisa Santiago, 142 Waveland, Waveland 39576

Sue Thomas, 1607 Main Street, Columbus 39701

Jean Tolbert, P.O. Box 1002, Brookhaven 39601

Ann Turner, 6005 Woodhaven Road, Jackson 39204

Alice Warriner, Route 5, Box 242, Poplarville 39470

Missouri

Lois Banning, 1256 Sunset Drive, Columbia 65201

Sarah Bateman, 49 Wheeler, Ft. Leonard Wood 65473

Beverly Beckmeyer, Box 69, Eureka 63025

Donna R. Bowman, 312 N. Gex, LaPlata 63549

Linda Buckner, 1415 Waterford Court, Columbia 65201

Roberta Casida, 34 Steeplechase, St. Peters 63376

Kay Eberhardt, 305 Forrest Acres Drive, O'Tallon 63366

Judith Flowers, 6011 Gaitling Drive, St. Louis 63129

Natalie Groth, 463 Briarwyck Drive, Ballwin 63011

Averial Hartsock, 18 Northridge, St. Joseph 64506

Judy Jackson, 3311 Smidon, Springfield 65801

Margie Larson, Star Route 4, Box 201, Houston 65483

Patricia Lowry, 10609 Twilight, St. Louis 63128

Marianne McLafferty, 415 Golthe, Kirkwood 63122

Jane Meyer, 1820 W. McCarty, Jefferson 65101

Fae Montgomery, 206 S. Main, DeSoto 63020

Billie Jean Newcomb, 628 Woodland, Moberly 65270

Marjorie Packard, Route 4, Box 32, Cameron 64429

Judy Perkins, Route 2, Box 48, Bernie 63822

Burton L. Picht, 106 E. Illinois, Box 266, Kirksville 63501

Frankie Polleschultz, 18 Club Grounds S. Drive, Florrisant 63032

Becky Pollock, 115 Missouri, Charleston 63834

Debi Roberts, Route 1, Box 18, Hurdland 63547

Janice D. Rosenburg, 1704 Little Brennan Road, High Ridge 63049

Ann Russell, Route 9, Box 506–D, Springfield 65801

Lynn Sadler, 802 S. Fible, Kirksville 63501

Elizabeth Stevens, P.O. Box 26, Gravois Mills 65037

Joan Trant, 444 Briarwyck Drive, Ballwin 63011

Judith C. Wilken, 1502 S. Warren, Sedalia 65301

Susan Woods, 346 Cooperstown Drive, Chesterfield 63017

Katherine Yoss, 123 E. Fourth Street, Appleton City 64724

Diane Zimmermann, Route 2, Box 177C, Wentzville 63385

Montana

Karen Adams, Nine Mile Ranger Station, Huson 59846

Michele Tebay, Route 1, Whitehall 59859

Nebraska

Doris Cronin, 447 S. Fourth Street, Burwell 68823

155

Marilyn Dye, Route 8, Lincoln 68506
Mary Gillespie, 1334 N. Hickory, Wahoo 68066
Barbara F. Jorgensen, Route 1, Box 135, Cozad 69130
Coralen Keeler, Box 171, Arlington 68001
Donna Kruse, Route 2, Albion 68620
Marlene LaChapelle, 6623 Bedford Avenue, Omaha 68109
Val Milbourn, 2970 31st Avenue, Columbus 68601
Mildred Pagels, 1441 W. 12th Street, Fremont 68025
George Rasmussen, 2039 Fair Acre, Fremont 68025
Eleanor B. Schroer, No. 6 Meadowlark, Kearney 68847
Meryl Stortz, 530 Glenhaven Drive, Lincoln 68505
Irene Summers, 8053 Blondo, Omaha 68134
Alice A. Thompson, P.O. Box 6013, Lincoln 68506
Marjorie Thompson, Route 1, Archer 68816
Lois C. Tollefsen, 2005 13th Avenue, Kearney 68847
Jean Uerling, 1919 First Avenue, Scottsbluff 69361
Mildred Winkelbauer, Route 1, Norfolk 68701

Nevada
E. "Frankie" Brooks, 4184 Candle Berry Ct., Las Vegas 89103
Ivan Brooks, 4184 Candle Berry Ct., Las Vegas 89103
Chris Burkham, 952 Hillside Drive, Elko 89801
Zelia Mae Coleman, 3150 S. Decatur, Las Vegas 89102
Dawna Daniels, 701 McDonald Drive, Reno 89503
Kay Loudon, 2515 Pioneer Drive, Reno 89509
Gail Meyer, 3864 Chutney, Las Vegas 89121
Stephen Sadler, 1040 Keystone, Reno 89501

New Hampshire
Eva Hogan, Pine Hill Road, RFD 3, Nashua 03060
Barbara Madden, Route 109, Box 261, Melvin Village 03850
Evelyn V. Mazierz, 4 Tumblebrook Lane, Nashua 03060
Patricia M. Metivier, 2 Sandy Circle, Pelham 03076
Barbara Mone, 43 Charles Street, Farmington 03835
Marion Pond, RFD 1, Exeter 03833
Harriet Tucker, RFD 3, Box 65, Dover 03820
Frances Valley, 6 Sunset Drive, Sommersworth 03878

New Jersey
Sharon Blair, P.O. Box 172, Main Street, Califon 07830
Margaret Byrne, 59 Lenox Road, Summit 07901
Marion P. Castiglia, 106 Juniper Street, Burlington 08016
Libby Dalon, 25 West Hampton Street, Pemberton 08068
Faith Delevante, 52 Laurel Drive, Wayne 07470
Barbara Eng, 62 Old Post Road, Freehold 07728
Angel Forschino, 1 Willow Way, Wanaque 07465
Ruth Henshaw, 422 N. 16th Street, Kenilworth 07033
Bonnie Litorja, 59 Megill Circle, Eatontown 07724
Roberta Linn Miller, 645 Howard Avenue, Pitman 08071
Selma Sellers, 11 Forman Drive, Hamilton Square 08690
Kathleen Stingle, 1215 Wyndmoor Road, Cherry Hill 08034
Patricia Wehr, 16 Hinchman Avenue, Denville 07834
Isabell Wiss, 291 Ridge Road, North Arlington 07032

New Mexico
Barbara Bencimo, 300 Downtown Mall, Las Cruces 88001
Mary Gay Billingsley, 200 Capri Road, Las Cruces 88001

Ann Filkins, 8700 Supreme Court, Albuquerque 87111
B. J. Hooe, 1020 E. Amador, Las Cruces 88001
Katy Lindberg, Box 2125, Farmington 87401
Eve LaTulipe, General Delivery, Cannon AFB 88101
Patsy Liston, Route 1, Box 130, Clovis 88101
Ida Moon, Box 673, Mesilla Park 88047
Eleanor Simpson, 817 Crestview, Farmington 87401

New York
Irene Adams, 842 Forest Avenue, Fulton 13069
Lynn Boink, 716 Oswego Street, Liverpool 13088
Betty Breen, 111 Shoreway Drive, Rochester 14612
Mary DiVirgilio, 311 Vandervoort Street, N. Tonawanda 14120
Yvonne Dugan, 8473 N. Main, Eden 14057
Linda Fanniff, 30 Manchester Drive, Clifton Park 12056
Estelle M. Hawkins, 16 Beechwood Avenue, Ballston 12019
Rita Hill, Box 177, Pennsylvania Avenue, Apalachin 13732
Jean Imgamells, 3278 S. Creek Road, Hamburg 14075
Concetta Katusak, 1048 Schuyler Street, Endicott 13760
Shirley M. Kent, 7656 E. Dead Creek Road, Baldwinsville 13027
Paula Lawton, RD 2, Box 8R, Valatie 12184
Jean Linnard, 39 Brookwood Drive, Latham 12110
Dianne Longmuir, 113 E. Bloomfield Street, Rome 13440
Sylvia Mannis, 8292 Adams Road, S. Glen Falls 12801
Karen Marz, 4864 Juneway Drive, So., Liverpool 13088
Ann Murphy, 3560 Carmen Road, Middleport 14105
Dottie Phillips, 7 Buffalo South, Corning 14830
Mary Pysz, 27 Donald Drive, North Tonawanda 14120
Laurrel D. Sahagian, 144 Consaul Road, Albany 12205
Peg Schisler, 9 Caveson Lane, Albany 12205
Betty Severtson, RD 5, Jamestown 14701
Janet Snell, 1273 Pembroke Court, Schenectady 12309
M. Veronica Stowell, No. 1 W. First Street, Fulton 13069
Shea Szachara, 2850 Vestal Parkway, W. Vestal 13732

North Carolina
Paulette Adams, 1720 H. Franciscan, Winston-Salem 27107
Shari Strong Bonham, 313 Carswell Lane, Goldsboro 27530
Regina Crook, Route 4, Monroe 28110
Louise Edward, 508 S. Pine, Rocky Mounts 27801
Jimmie Evans, Star Route, Bat Cave 28710
Barbara Hanson, 1675 Glengarry Drive, Cary 27511
Loretta House, 2853 Reynolds Road NW, Winston Salem 27106
Alice Johnson, P.O. Box 1029, Shelby 28150
Adelaide C. Monds, 310 W. Dicive Street, Dunn 28334
Alice Morales, Route 5, Box 169C, Monroe 28110
Patty Norwood, 1208 Dove Street, Monroe 28110
Nita B. Phillips, 4310 Shipyard Boulevard, Wilmington 28401
Lee Schandler, 50 Broadway, Asheville 28807
Beth M. Smith, 310½ West Divine, Dunn 28334
Mary Spainhour, Box 141, Pinnocle 27043
Carolyn Sproles, 4310 Shipyard Boulevard, Wilmington 28401
Mildred Whittington, 612 S. Cannon Boulevard, Kannapolis 28081

North Dakota
Judi Braasch, R.R. 1, Jamestown 58401

Lavern Burke, Box 814, Devils Lake 58301
Penny R. Frey, Route 1, Jamestown 58401
Agnes Leik, 812 Central Avenue, New Rockford 58356
Linda Lennie, 708 No. 21st Street, Bismarck 58501
Laura Quaglia, 132–2 Delta Drive, Minot 58704
Susan Stinar, 1601 North Third Street, Grand Forks 58201

Ohio
Audrey Aeschbacher, 1112 Mt. Vernon Avenue, Marion 43302
Pattie Anderson, 3163 Easton Road, Norton 44203
Mildred W. Beacham, 11822 Glenfalls Cincinnati 45246
Margaret M. Beard, 2400 Mechanicsburg Road, Springfield 45503
Jeanne Beckman, 3696 Meridian Road, Youngstown 44501
Sylvia Bosserman, 623 Spring Street, Covington 45318
Marge Brown, 6952 Gettysburg Drive, Sylvania 43560
Bonnie Burkholder, 175 W. Third, Mansfield 44901
Elaine Clark, 1589 Berkshire Road, Columbus 43216
Sophie Crawford, 8406 Winston Road, Cincinnati 45202
Anna Croushore, 5165 Fishburg Road, Dayton 45401
Carole Donnelly, 6680 Woodsedge Drive, Reynoldsburg 43068
Erika Fedderke, 1 Zimmerman Court, Defiance 43512
Marguerite Fratus, 79 Claren Drive, Heath 43055
Betty Garratt, 1300 Shrine Road, Box 147, Springfield 44501
Sara Grove, 26 W. Broad Street, Newton Falls 44444
Patricia Grubb, 3256 Bradford, Cleveland Heights 44118
Doris Hagensick, 2442 Northbranch Road, Grove City 43123
Alice Hall, 6787 Shurz Road, Middleton 45042
Betty Hidy, 123 E. Main Street, Donnelsville 45319
Carol Hoffman, 111 E. McPherson Highway, Clyde 43410
Ginny Holtgreven, 1207 Nicklin Avenue, Pigua 45356
Amber Horst, 300 Grant Street, Wooster 44691
Mary Jarnagin, 5915 Gilmore Drive, Fairfield 45014
Deborah Jessee, 811 Picket Way, Cincinnati 45245
Peggy Ann Jessee, 823 Picket Way, Cincinnati 45245
Lois Knight, 2901 Lookout Drive, Zanesville 43701
Agnes J. Kulchock, 826 Bonnie Brae NE, Warren 44484
Jo Lamancusa, 565 Broadway, Bedford 44139
Lea Lewis, 518 Lake Avenue, Lakeview 45331
Loraine Lockard, Clyde 43410
Carol D. Martin, 84 Day Avenue, Newark 43055
Normagene Martin, 1474 W. State, Route 718, Troy 45373
Lois Maxwell, 1111 Overlook, Alliance 44601
JoAnn McDevitt, 1672 Ranch Road, East Palestine 44413
Margarette McDonnell, 380 Mt. Vernon Road, Newark 43055
Nancy Mohr, 39215 Detroit Road, Avon 44011
Judi Myers, 403 Red Rock Drive, Wadsworth 44281
Tina Norris, 3567 S. Ridge, Perry 44081
Nadine Oldfield, 5360 Vandemark Road, Medina 44256
Barbara Pancost, 8124 Main Street, Chagrin Falls 44022
Patricia Paul, 930 Valley View Drive, Brookfield 44403

Sara Payne, 148 High Street, Chagrin Falls 44022

Virginia Phillips, 140 N. Wright Street, Yellow Springs 45387

Jacqueline Pollack, 4116 Kinsey Road, Englewood 45322

Sharon Putman, 128 Tolowa Trail, Lina 45802

Nancy Richardson, 3104 Bonnie Villa, Lane Dayton 45431

Paula Robinson, 2536 Valleywood Avenue NE, Massillon 44646

Marjorie Savely, 100 W. North Street, Waverly 45690

Barbara Schultz, 269 Hager Street, Hubbard 44425

Jane Seelig, 24 N. State Street, Westerville 43081

Sharon D. Shafer, 330 S. Blanchard, Findlay 45840

Marlo Sigler, 103 S. Main Street, Union 45322

Terry Smith, 12554 Harold Drive, Chesterland, 44026

Marjorie Spahr, 585 Highland Park Drive, Akron 44310

Virginia L. Smith, 1791 Douglas Avenue, Monroe 45050

Mary Lou Stewart, 967 Thomas Drive, Ashland 44805

Barbara A. Sturgeon, 701 Crestmont Drive, Dayton 45431

Betty Sweeney, 1509 S. Fourth, Ironton 45638

Janice Thomas, 3696 S. Meridian Road, Youngstown 44501

Fran Thompson, 680 Martha Drive SE, Vienna 44473

Cyndi Townsend, 8588 Center Street, Garretsville 44231

Evelyn Vicol, 4424 N. Rodge W., Ashtabula 44004

Sharon Voelker, 1349 W. Lane Avenue, Columbus 43212

Rita Warner, 4105 Albon Road, Mondova 43542

Shirley Warren, Route 1, Lakeview 43331

Marge Wennerstrom, 5864 Mayfield Road, Cleveland 44101

Kathy White, P.O. Box 75, Lakeview 43331

Martha L. Wick, 4511 Frederick Road, Dayton 45401

Carolyn Wolfe, 434 Whirrlesey Drive, Tallmadge 44278

Grace A. Woods, P.O. Box 142, Millersburg 44654

Lois Wyant, 331 E. Lytle Five Point Road, Dayton 45401

Floris Zimmerman, 236 W. Liberty Street Wooster 44691

Oklahoma

Alice Bearden, 1307 Hickory, Duncan 73533

Marilyn J. Belyeu, WSR Box 260 A, Checotah 74426

Jean N. Betler, 420 N. 11th, Fairview 73737

Debby Boss, 9705 S. 235 E. Avenue, Broken Arrow 74012

Nita Campbell, 9424 East 40th Place, Tulsa 74145

Carolyn Coffman, 1508 Ash, Muskogee 74401

Beckye Conklin, 29 N. Gum, Altus AFB 73521

Mary Anne Cosper, 2915 So. 95th E. Avenue, Tulsa 74129

Rose Cotner, Route 1, Bounds 74047

Carolyn Cox, Route 1, Box 252B, Duncan 73533

Jean Crider, Box 252, Perry 73077

Pat Crume, 621 N. Cherokee, Claremore 74017

Anna R. Dettweiler, Route 2, Box 214B, Watonga 73772

Gary Devine, 1418 N. Minnesota, Shawnee 74801

Doris Dodson, 3230 S. Florence, Tulsa 74105

Emily Donnelly, 2424 N.W. 118, Oklahoma City 73120

Leah M. Dunn, 820 South Sixth, Kingfisher 73950

Barbara Ellis, 5701 S. Rockford Place, Tulsa 74105

Phyllis Evans, Route 7, Box 179B, Claremore 74017

Jimi Ewing, 107 N. Main, Miami 75354

Carolyn Fedde, 4704 S. 70th E. Avenue, Tulsa 74145

Georga Funk, Route 1, Box 137, Coyle 73027

Shirley Gibbons, Route 6, Box 703, Guthrie 73044

Carole Gilliland, 4913 Bahama Avenue, Sand Springs 74063

Ellen Hill, Route 5, Box 83, Guthrie 73044

Helen Hill, 720 N. Oklahoma Street, Guymon 73942

Darlene Hughes, 301 West Sixth, Bristow 74010

LaVona Irwin, 6th & Georgia, Anadarko 73005

Donna Johnson, 12724 E. 137th Street, Broken Arrow 74012

Dorothy Johnson, 7041 E. 52nd Street, Tulsa 74135

Sharon Johnson, 13913 E. 27th Street, Tulsa 74134

Wanda Johnston, 1010 S. 6th Street, Ponca City 74601

Patricia C. Jones, 1907 N. York, Muskogee 74401

Melody Keane, 1845 S. 106 East Avenue, Tulsa 74128

Donna Keasling, 6420 S.E. Baylor Drive, Bartlesville 74003

Beula King, P.O. Box 370, Hugo 74743

Barbara Lancaster, 824 Delaware, Perry 73077

Xenia Lillard, 708 W. Sandy Road, Atoka 74525

Dorothy Linihan, 1112 S.E. 17th Street, Pryor 74361

Della Jean Littleton, Box 186, Custer City 73639

Phyllis Lynn, Route 2, Box 623, Broken Arrow 74012

Betty Mansur, 5417 S. 76th E. Avenue, Tulsa 74145

Vera McCoy, Route 5, Box 7, McAlester 74501

Wendy McCoy, Route 1, Box 99, Wilburton 74578

Mary McDermitt, 118 A. Street, N.W. Ardmore 73401

Janie Medina, 2604 S.W. 90th, Oklahoma City 73159

Naomi Meeks, 2676 S. Richmond, Tulsa 74114

Nell Miller, P.O. Box 366, Boswell 74727

Shelby Miller, 3116 Briarwood, Bethany 73008

Rita Ann Mitchell, 305 South Sixth, Broken Arrow 74012

Betty Morgan, 200 S. 15th, Frederick 73542

Hazel Moseley, Route 1, Box 18, Mannford 74044

Sondra Mullins, 7030 East 77th, Tulsa 74133

Chris Myer, 1429 E. 38th Street, Tulsa 75105

Kathy Oldham, 1318 W. Cherokee, Enid 73701

Mildred Patterson, 501 E. Oklahoma, Guthrie 73044

Jennie Pease, P.O. Box 158, Alderson 74522

Greer Peters, 1131 B. Kilbreth Place, Ft. Sill 73503

Carrol Piel, 601 Delaware Street, Perry 73077

Tina Lee Plummer, 1300 Oxford Way, Route 3, Anadarko 73005

Rosetta Preston, 7502 S. 70th Avenue, Tulsa 74133

Edith Ramsey, 412 N. Sawyer, Pryor 74361

Faye Rikkola, 804 N. Elm Street, Owasso 74055

Shirley Rosamund, Route 2, Box 470, Broken Arrow 74012

Juanita Scott, 1204 N. Vandalia, Tulsa 74145

Sue Sensintaffar, 705 W. Canton Avenue, Broken Arrow 74012

LaTasha Sharry, Route 1, Box 28, Colony 73021

Lisa Ann Smith, 8944 E. 57th Street, Tulsa 74145

Jewell Snyder, Route 3, Box 159DD, Altus 73521

Sue Spiva, 117 W. Seventh, Stillwater 74074

Martha Taylor, 1105 N.W. 16th, Lawton 73501

Libby Volker, 1038 E. 35th Place, Tulsa 74105

Esther G. Wymer, 512 N. Eighth, Fairview 73737

Helen Young, Box 6, Manchester 73758

Oregon

Judy Bell, 250 S.E. Ventura Place, Bend 97702

Linda Fast, 3347 Storey Boulevard, Eugene 97405

Dona Goodfellow, 525 N.W. Third, Ontario 97914

Elaine Killebrew, Box 626, Ontario 97914

Trudy Lynn Locks, P.O. Box 803, Roseburg 97470

Donna Santos, 4438 N.E. 131 Place, Portland 97208

Harold Seley, 166 S. Oregon, Ontario 97914

Dorothy Stout, 970 Airport Road, Lebanon 97355

Mildred Stuwe, 1105 Savage Road, N.E., Salem 97301

Barbara Youngers, 4466 Viewcrest Road, So. Salem 97302

Pennsylvania

Betty Badgley, 38 Bittersweet Drive, Glen Mills 19243

Julie Bazewicz, 1212 E. 6th Street, Berwick 18603

Faye R. Benett, 3423 Kutztown Road, Laureldale 19065

Gloria Brosious, 6518 Rising Sun Avenue, Philadelphia 19111

Charmaine Cesar, 714 Mt. Avenue, Pen Aigul 18072

Jean Deitrick, P.O. Box B, Benton 17814

Patricia Diestrich, 100 Roosevelt Avenue, McKees Rocks 15136

Lynda Dotterer, 1131 Ferris Avenue, Berwick 18603

Sharon B. Drewfs, U.S. Army War College, Carlisle Bks 17013

Ruth Edwards, Box 302 Main Street, Schaefferstown 17088

Ruth Eitel, 1726 Ridgewood Drive, Washington 15301

Dorothy M. Falcone, 508 English Road, Bath 18014

Bee Figuly, 2540 Blossom Lane, New Castle 16105

Billie H. Fleming, 384 New Castle Road, Butler 16001

Pepper Aubrey George, 2915 Whitewood Road, Bethleham 18016

Gloria Jones, 112 Stump Road, North Wales 19454

Rella L. Keller, 790 Joy Drive, Greencastle 17225

Geri King, 1798 Davison Road, Harborcreek 16421

Elinor Meyer, P.O. Box 703, Doylestown 18901

Carol Myer, 1000 W. Ingomar Road, Pittsburgh 15237

Phillip Myer, St. James House 902, 13th & Walnut Streets, Philadelphia 19107

Edith Nelson, 312 Belmont Avenue, Mt. Pocono 18344

Carol Peters, 3665 Backus Road, Harborcreek 16421

Kay Probst, R.D. 1, Stillwater 17878

JoAnn B. Schlosser, 137 Ensminger, Jacobus 17407

Ruth Schrader, 539 Reagan Street, Sunbury 17801

Janice D. Sherman, 3595 Brownsville Road, Pittsburgh 15227

Gail Snaman, 855 Bridgewater Drive, Pittsburgh 15216

Pamela H. Stine, 5A Colonial Crest Circle, Hanover 17331

Glendora B. Vanorden, 100 Shady Lane, Carlisle 17013

Rita Weeks, 1705 Crestview Avenue, Willow Grove 19090

Betty Witmer, P.O. Box 84, Mt. Holly Springs 17065

Rhode Island

Cheryl V. Merolla, 567 Putnam Pike, Greenville 02828

Jeanne Serpa, 31 Johnson Avenue, Narragansett 02882

157

South Carolina

Betty Agnew, 612 Lyman Street, Gaffney 29340

Peggy Anderson, 1203 Collins Park Street, Conway 29526

Juanita Brouillette, 146 Bailey Avenue, Rock Hill 29730

Launa Cramer, 10 Woodmont Circle, Greenville 19602

Margaret D. Howison, 299 Plantation Road, Rock Hill 29730

John E. Howison, 299 Plantation Road, Rock Hill 29730

Mildred Knight, 405 Woodland Drive, Lancaster 29720

Judith C. Lawing, 605 Jasmine Avenue, Myrtle Beach 29577

Liz Newman, 1241 A. Walnut, Myrtle Beach 29577

Renee Powell, 1721 Ashley Hall Road, Apt 1T, Charleston 19407

Jo Schwartz, 208 Devon Drive, Mauldin 19662

Charlene Youngblood, P.O. Box 2794, Myrtle Beach 29577

South Dakota

Elsie Colerick, 2016 Selkirk Place, Rapid City 57701

Millie Ericksen, 609 E. Fourth, Colten 57018

Delores Rudd, 805 N. Main, Sioux Falls 57705

Donna Suther, 903 Third Street, Britton 57430

Tennessee

Edith Beaty, 400 Green Acres, Memphis 38117

Lou Breeding, 202 South First, Union City 38261

Barbara Brownlee, 3203 Austin Peay Highway, Memphis 38101

Martha Brewer, 2751 Stage Park Drive, Memphis 38134

Georgia Buckner, 1719 Old Lascossas Road, Murfreesboro 37310

Nancy Bowie Carter, 915 Anderson Street, Bristol 37620

Mary Frances Collins, Route 2, Box 422, Camden 38320

Barbara Decker, Northdate Mall, Tallahoma 37388

Jane Dryden, 2033 North Locust, P.O. Box 336, Lawrenceburg 38464

Helen Dunham, 209 Lane Oak Road, Concord 37720

Margaret Grace, 4752 Linda Lane, Memphis 38117

Ann Gray, 3933 Wisteria, Memphis 38116

Frieda Hamm, 144 Cypress Avenue, Selmer 39375

Cathy Johnson, 4036 Beechdale Cove, Memphis 38128

Cornelia M. Judd, 5001 Bell Road Q1, Hermitage 37076

Joyce Longworth, 11024 Thorton Drive, Knoxville 37922

Betty Maier, 3930 Patte Ann Drive, Memphis 38116

Patty McKnight, 7666 Highway 51 N., Millington 38053

Ide Lee Parkman, 5855 Park Avenue, Chatham Village, Memphis 38138

Suzy Ramsey, 4525 Old Stage Road, Kingsport 37614

Margaret Rosenbloom, 63 Summar Drive, Jackson 38301

Rieta Selberg, 2020 Whispering Pines, Germantown 38138

Joan Stamper, 123 Franklin, P.O. Box 415, Clarksville 38053

Marjory Stumpenhorst, Route 1, Sharon Lane, Jackson 38301

Karen M. Tate, 1520 Central Avenue, Memphis 38104

Evelyn Welty, Route 7, Box 252, Lebanon 37087

Ann Williams, 1900 Randolph Place, Nashville 37202

Dot York, P.O. Box 1765, 816 Lakeside Drive, Fairfield Glade 38555

Texas

Elaine Adamek, Route 5, Box 261-X, Victoria 77901

Anita Annucci, 2607 Amherst Drive, Wichita Falls 76308

Nancy Atkison, 108 Saint Jo Terrace, Nocona 76255

Noreen Banes, 2707 Albert, Carrollton 75077

J. Ann Bauerkemper, 613 Sky Forest, San Antonio 78232

Marge Bernholz, 2123 Ridgemore Drive, Houston 77070

Mary Ann Bowie, 707 N. 8th Street, Longview 75601

Marilyn Bradley, 2032 Houston Place, Denton 76201

Rosa Brashier, Route 1, Box 254, Hillsboro 76645

Pat Brass, 5010 Spencer, Pasadena 77501

Miriam Brooks, 8342 San Fernando Way, Dallas 75218

Kathryn Buckley, 101 Oakhurst Drive, Palestine 75801

Grace Bulla, 907 Charles, Panhandle 79068

Gretchen Cagle, 2909 Haymeadow, Carrolton 76436

Peggy Caldwell, 62 Meyer Road, Huffman 77336

Edith Childrey, 264 Dijon, Leander 78641

Edwina Cline, 2627 Albans, Houston 77005

Essie Cole, 2708 Morrow, Corpus Christi 78410

Melida Coleman, Box 1037, Laredo 78040

Becky Connally, 141 Medallion Center, Dallas 75320

Hazel Corbett, P.O. Box 868, Dalhart 79022

Maliza W. Cox, 3112 Drexel Drive, Dallas 75205

Susette Davenport, P.O. Box 415, Brenham 77833

Mary Margaret DeHart, 2803 Burnt Oak, San Antonio 78232

Nettie Lee Dinn, 335 Oak Glen, San Antonio 78206

Jackie Dodge, 27170 Afton Way, Huffman 77336

Mary Domec, Route 1, Box 84-K, Jasper 75951

Cindy Dunagan, 2009 W. Eighth, Ft. Stockton 79735

Selena Earle, 302 Milton, Jacksonville 75766

Johnnye Echols, 5030 Crusade Drive, San Antonio 78206

Vicky Eidson, 2301 E. Highway 83, Donna 78537

Barbara Epperson, 4107 Birdwell Drive, Tyler 75701

Loraine Fears, 208 Richmond, Angleton 77515

Shirley M. Gaultney, 806 Finale, San Antonio 78216

Carol Gerk, Route 4, Box 42, Herford 79045

Barbara Gibson, Box 983, Kilgore 75662

Ruth Gooch, 812 E. 4th, Denver City 79323

Edith Green, 1208 Tarnerick Drive, Mexia 76667

Ruth Hancock, 100 W. Walnut, Decatur 76234

Viola Hardgrave, Route 5, Box 301, Palestine 75801

Milly Haring, 315 N. Travis, Sherman 75090

Connie Harvis, 6261 Goliad Apt. A, Dallas 75214

Bernice Haynes, P.O. Box 565, Dickinson 77539

Ruth Heasley, Box 683, Fulton 78358

Ann Heck, 111 Woodbine Drive, Palestine 75801

Mary Henry, P.O. Box 1693, Plainview 79072

Ginney Hernlund, 5818 Burnett Road, Austin 78767

Mary Ellen Hillis, 201 W. Niblick, Longview 75604

Winnie Hinger, 3833 Ridgeoak, Dallas 75234

Betty Holladay, 1201 Adams Street, Conroe 77301

Jo Hollingsworth, 720 E. Corsicana, Athens 75751

Mary Houlette, 910 N.E. 4th, Dumas 79029

Jean Jennings, 3024 N. Vernon, Amarillo 79107

Beth Johnston, Route 2, Box 217B, Palestine 75801

Barbara Jones, 1115 Central Boulevard, Brownsville 78520

June Jones, Route 1, Box 105D, Rockwall 75087

Shirley Jones, 559 Patricia, San Antonio 78216

Nina Judd, 419 N. Maple, Stratford 77477

Annie May Jurcak, 909 W. 12th Street, Plainview 79072

Delores Leach, 8008 Seawall Boulevard, No. 240, Galveston 77551

Mary Lewis, 2279 Triway Lane, Houston 77701

Mrs. O.B. Livingston, 600 E. Main, Nacogdoches 75961

Jeanette Lukeman, 803 Attow, Brenham 77833

Martha McLean, 3302 Pleasant Grove Road, Texarkana 75501

Kathi McKinzie, 305 Zephyr, Plainview 79072

Ruth Medaris, 2312 South, Kilgore 75662

Charlotte Miller, 1306 Sandy Circle, Irving 75060

Theresa Milton, 2607 Amherst Drive, Wichita Falls 76308

Irene Moore, 112 Meadbrook, Palestine 75801

Margaret Morgan, 620 Donna Lane, Bedford 76021

Nora Beth Morton, Throckmorton 76083

Jamie Murray, 720 N. Downing, Angleton 77515

Gina Musick, 215 E. 43rd, Odessa 79760

Eva Nixon, 2654 34th, Lubbock 79408

Betty Partridge, 1702 Lexington, Deer Park 77536

Martha Penland, 117 Cedar Heights, Palestine 75801

Rose Ann Pool, 3419 Pearl Street, Nacogdoches 75961

Mona Post, 15907 Echo Hill Drive, Clear Lake City 77059

Nancy Posz, 201 N. Eighth, Killeen 76541

Jo Pratt, 26842 45th Street, Spring 77373

Sonja Rumsey, 209 Forbush, San Antonio 78206

Margaret Silar, 303 S. Ross, Mexia 76667

Audrey Smith, 4242 S. Fifth, Abilene 79065

Angie Stephen, 1903 Signet, Euless 76039

Mary Stewart, S. Plain Mall B13, Lubbock 79414

Jan Sursa, Route 2, Box 2154, Boerne 78006

Alvia Theilg, 5430 Chenna, Houston 77096

Audrey Tweed, 324 White Rock N. Shopping Center, Dallas 75238

Flo Viles, 4801 Roberts Drive, Lewisville 75056

Betty Walker, 11526 Walf Run, Houston 77701

Joanne J. Webb, 5318 Hemlock, Baytown 77521

Barbara West, 3713 Dartmouth, Garland 75043

Betty Westcott, P.O. Box 1047, Livingston 77351

Ann Williams, 79 Outer Octagon, Randolph AFB 78148

Pat Wheeler, 108 N. Crescent, Electra 76360

Janice Wilson, 229 Lomont, El Paso 79951

Adaline Wittie, 1240 Rice Road, San Antonio 78220

Claudine Wolfe, 1210 Cedar, Kileen 76541

Utah

Catherine Allen, 1332 N. 1580 West, Farmington 84025

Betty Headman, 1082 590 E., Orem 84057

Sharon Peterson, 58 W. Gentile, Layton 84041

Eleanor Zimmerman, P.O. Box 7620, Salt Lake City 84110

Kim Zimmerman, 4370 S. 300 West, Salt Lake City 84110

Vermont

Muriel A. Bohne, Harwood Hill, Bennington 05201

Val Steele, R.R. 2, Box 175, Windsor 05089

Virginia

Janet Bowen, 235 Arrowhead Trail, Christiansburg 24073

Penny Carroll, 4412 Ben Franklin, Virginia Beach 23462

Jo Cormier, 10347 Hampshire Green Avenue, Fairfax 22032

Diane Theresa Dodd, 12156 Holly Knoll Circle, Great Falls 22066

Emma Duncan, 7439 Major Avenue, Norfolk 23505

June B. Garrison, 2605 River Oaks Drive, Chesapeake 23321
Janet Goldbach, 2123 Hollybriar Point, Norfolk 23518
Anne Higgins, 2038 Plank Road, Fredericksburg 22401
Mary Lu Hollerbach, 5009 Finn Road, Virginia Beach 23455
Mary Jo Jennings, Box 3070, Martinsville 24112
Rena Kramer, 121 Twin Creek Terrace, Forest 24551
Diane Lane, 404 Johnstown Road, Chesapeake 23320
Betty J. Leary, Route 3, Box 180A, Amherst 24521
Jane Ludwig, 300 Homeplace Drive, Salem 25153
Jane Rickman, 7218 Hadlow Drive, Springfield 22150
Janet Ryburn, 104 Franklin Street, Blue Field 24605
Rosemarie Schwindt, 2408 Heutte Drive, Norfolk 23501
Roslyn Stallcup, 1436 Lakeview Drive, Virginia Beach 23462
Elizabeth Tush, 1608 Chatham Road, Waynesboro 22980

Washington
Hazel Behar, 4803 Ahtanum Road, Yakima 98901
Jane Carroll, H89 N. 100 Irving Place, Kennewick 99336
Shirley Charette, 7713 47th West, Tacoma 98466
Margaret J. Dillard, 1220 Mt. Whitney Dr., Vancouver 98664
Kaye Miller, 416 Sudden Valley, Bellingham 98225
Allegra Sampson, 518 W. Entiat Avenue, Kennewick 99336
Barbara Williams, 405 S. Buntin, Kennewick 99336

West Virginia
Shirley Hortsman, 508 McNeill Avenue, Point Pleasant 25550
Dorothy B. Neal, 3147 Saltwell Road, Huntington 25701
Sue Persinger, 121 Watson Avenue, Shrewsbury 25184

Juanita Redmond, Box 324, Boomer 25031
Virginia Sue Sharps, RD No. 4, Bello-Vedere, Wheeling 26003

Wisconsin
Rose M. Ault, 340 N. Military Avenue, Green Bay 54303
Elizabeth Brudos, 307 Kertzman Place, La-Crosse 54601
Kathy Geis, R.R. 4, Fond du Lac 54935
Norma Harrington, 1101 W. Ganville Road, Mequon 53092
Patti Hepburn, 1070 E. Thorn Lane, Milwaukee 53217
Molly Hoople, 290 Doty Street, Fond du Lac 54935
Eleanor Little, Box 209, Main Street, LaValle 53941
Anabelle Perry, 956 Valentine Road, Oconomowoc 53066
Rose Rosenberg, 810 E. Grant, Eau Claire 54701
Martha Jane Schult, Route 2, LaCrosse 54601
Bob Smith, 7940 W. Layton Avenue, Milwaukee 53220

Wyoming
Marietta Armstrong, 1823 E. 17th Street, Cheyenne 82001
Eleanor Hewgley, 1116 Cactus Hill Road, Cheyenne 82001
Claudie Meyer, Box 236, Pinedale 82941
Delchia Neighbors, Box 230, Sheridan 82801
Barbara Ullrich, 768 Ranger, Cheyenne 82001

Canada
Barbara Bassett, 615 Lansdowne, Westmount H3Y 2V7
Maureen Berlin, 3880 198th Street, BC
Martine Cheval, 20 Mississaugh Valley Boulevard, Mississaugh, Ontario L5A 3S1
Helen Cockshutt, 96 Merdine Circle, London, Ontario N5X 1G2
Kathleen Dunn, 4 McRarle Avenue, Atikokan, Ontario P0T 1C0
Barbara Edney, R.R. 1, Churchill, Ontario L0L 1K0
Delma Green, 5 Pine Street, Dartmouth, Nova Scotia B2Y 3Z3
Beverly Helzinger, 5038 Sherbrooke St. W., Montreal, Quebec

Barbara Kaufman, 52 Graydon Street, London, Ontario
Kate Mallin, 236 Kingston Row, Winnepeg, Manitoba R2M 0T4
Helen J. Marchyn, 127 Lock Hart Drive, St. Catharines, Ontario L2T 1W3
Sally McLaren, 6050 Wyandotte Street, E. Windsor, Ontario
Janice Montreul, 524 Charon, Montreal Quebec H3K 2P5
Janet Murdoch, 705 Gilbert Road, Richmond, BC
Audrey Neale, 85 Brittany Avenue, Town of Mt. Royal, PQ
Vera Newman, 308 Centre Street, Essex, Ontario
Gail Perks, 17 O'Hara Drive, Halifax, Nova Scotia B3M 2E8
Sharon Predy, 4975 Westminster Avenue, Delta, BC V4K 2J1
Brigitte Roseman, 35 Cedarland Drive, Brantford, Ontario
Linda J. Seely, Box 333, Stirling, Alberta T0K 2E0
Valerie Skemp, 593 Egret Court, Richmond, BC V7F 3W2
Ruth Smith, R.R. 1, Wilmont, Nova Scotia B0P 1N0
Leona Taylor, 6355 E. Broadway, N. Burnaby, BC
Marilynn Van Zant, 12327 Lake Moraine, Calgary, Alberta
Bernice Wishart, 264 Varsity Cres. N.W., Alberta T3B 226
Kathy Woolsey, 2842 Heath Drive, Victoria, BC V9A 2J5

Finland
Sari Numi, Mellstinun, 9F3, 02170, Espor 17

Saudi Arabia
Nancy Rano, c/o Arabian CBI, P.O. Box 208, Yanbu

South Africa
Diane Faktor, 17 Verbenia, Pretoria 0081
Ann Fine, P.O. Box 1223, Kempton Park, 1620, Transvaal

Index